Jazz Age Cocktails

HISTORY, LORE, *and* RECIPES *from* AMERICA'S ROARING TWENTIES

Cecelia Tichi

WASHINGTON MEWS BOOKS
An Imprint of
NEW YORK UNIVERSITY PRESS
New York

NEW YORK UNIVERSITY PRESS
New York
www.nyupress.org

© 2021 by New York University
All rights reserved

References to Internet websites (URLs) were accurate at the time of writing.
Neither the author nor New York University Press is responsible for URLs
that may have expired or changed since the manuscript was prepared.

Library of Congress Cataloging-in-Publication Data
Names: Tichi, Cecelia, 1942– author.
Title: Jazz age cocktails : history, lore, and recipes from America's roaring twenties /
Cecelia Tichi.
Description: New York : New York University Press, [2021] | Series: Washington mews |
Includes bibliographical references and index.
Identifiers: LCCN 2021015238 | ISBN 9781479810123 (hardback) |
ISBN 9781479810130 (ebook) | ISBN 9781479810154 (ebook other)
Subjects: LCSH: Cocktails—United States. |
United States—Social life and customs—20th century.
Classification: LCC TX951 .T4923 2021 | DDC 641.87/4—dc23
LC record available at https://lccn.loc.gov/2021015238

New York University Press books are printed on acid-free paper, and their
binding materials are chosen for strength and durability. We strive to
use environmentally responsible suppliers and materials to
the greatest extent possible in publishing our books.

Manufactured in the United States of America

10 9 8 7 6 5 4 3 2 1

Also available as an ebook

CONTENTS

Introduction: A Jazz Age Cocktail   1

1 The Cocktail Hour   9

2 Criminal Intent   19

3 Ballyhoo: The Modern Moment   39

4 Newest New Woman   47

5 All That Jazz   57

6 Slinging Slang   65

7 *Génération perdue*   71

8 Wheels   80

9 Rum-Runners, Rum Row, and the Real McCoy   83

10 Bootlegging Ladies   93

11 Drink, Drank, Drunk   99

12 Winging It   103

13 Harry's New York Bar, Paris   115

14 The Silver Screen   119

15 A "Dry" Christmas   130

16 In the Money (While It Lasts)   136

17 The Party's Over   142

Acknowledgments   145

Bibliography   149

Index of Cocktails   157

About the Author   159

INTRODUCTION

A JAZZ AGE COCKTAIL

Nineteen-twenties America—the "Roaring Twenties"—boasted any number of famous *firsts*: the passage of the Nineteenth Amendment in August 1920, which at last gave American women the right to vote; Charles Lindbergh's solo flight across the Atlantic Ocean in May 1927; the explosive popularity of jazz music and talking motion pictures; and an array of powerful new vehicles from Ford, General Motors, and Chrysler, the "Big Three" automakers, who produced models in modish colors and a sleek, lowered silhouette. The decade saw baseball surge in popularity to become America's favorite sport as celebrity athlete George Herman ("Babe") Ruth, Jr., the New York Yankees' own "Sultan of Swat," slammed record-breaking home runs (sixty in the 1927 season alone). The stock market hit its own booming "home runs" as Wall Street speculators, fueled by bank loans, bought shares on margin, a practice followed by the faithful of Main Street, who trusted their brokers to deliver untold riches. American retailers, meanwhile, offered wondrous and time-saving devices like the safety razor, the electric vacuum cleaner, and, for the affluent and aspiring public, the Ciné-Kodak, a home movie camera. The privations of the First World War were over, industry geared up, and a vast new array of manufactured goods flowed to eager consumers.

The decade opened, nonetheless, with a resounding shock. On Friday, January 16, 1920, the Eighteenth Amendment became the law of the land. First introduced in Congress in 1917 and nicknamed the Volstead Act after the Honorable Andrew John Volstead (b. 1860), a Republican legislator from Granite Falls, Minnesota, who steered it through Congress, the National Prohibition Act made it illegal "to manufacture, sell, barter, transport, import, export, deliver, furnish or possess any intoxicating liquors." Once it had been ratified by the states two years later, America had officially gone "dry."

On its face, the well-organized and dogged temperance movement, dating from the 1850s, had triumphed at long last. The Anti-Saloon League and the Women's Christian Temperance Union and their allies had prevailed in their campaign to demonize alcoholic beverages, ridding America of "John Barleycorn" while promising a spiritually cleansed nation. The so-called Golden Age of Cocktails, which had risen with America's fortunes since the 1870s, was slated for certain doom. The mahogany bars that had held countless Manhattans, Ramos Gin Fizzes, hot toddies, and a host of other effervescent cocktails, along with the Gilded Age alchemists who had concocted the seductive drinks, would be abandoned as relics of a besotted past.

No sooner had the calendar page turned, however, than American ingenuity rose to its newest challenge. Countless cocktails, wines, "spiked" punches, and liqueurs had been a welcome part of American social and business life for the past half-century, and imbibers were not to be denied. The Volstead law, when scrutinized, proved to be riddled with loopholes, and the parched citizenry of the nation looked to a new generation of entrepreneurs to chart an illicit but "spirited" distribution network that let intoxicants flow to every hamlet and metropolis throughout the country.

The backwoods moonshiners' stills, plucked from rustic folklore, grew to become big business, and thirsty Americans welcomed the smuggled contraband liquors that were shipped in vessels flagged from foreign shores. (Offloaded in the dark of night, the cargo was seldom intercepted along the twelve thousand miles of Atlantic, Pacific, and Gulf coasts, not to mention shorelines of the Great Lakes, rivers, and the land borders.) Gangland lords, notably Chicago's Alphonse Gabriel ("Al") Capone, eluded the federal revenue agents and flaunted their wealth in expensive suits and bulletproof Cadillacs. Though the newly appointed Prohibition commissioner, John F. Kramer, announced to the press that "liquor used as a beverage must not be . . . hauled in anything on the surface of the earth or under the earth," the brazen hauling continued, unstopped and unstoppable, until the Eighteenth Amendment was repealed in 1933. According to Charles Merz's *The Dry Decade* (1930), law enforcement found Prohibition to be "a more complex, arduous, and debilitating experience than had been anticipated."

The 1920s wrote a new, distinct chapter in the nation's saga of spirits, with a vocabulary matching its modern moment. Men and women spoke knowingly of the speakeasy and the faithful dispenser of alcohol, the bootlegger, the name no longer limited to a flask tucked into a rustic moonshiner's boot, but now applied to the industrial-scale production of moonshine and rum-running, to black ships, blind pigs, gin mills, and gallon stills. For home consumption, "medicinal" whiskey or gin could be sought at the local drugstore (leading to an explosion of drugstore chains across the nation) or in the back room of an ice cream parlor, while such passwords as "Oscar sent me" and presentation of membership cards—21 Club, New Stork Club, Club Entre Nous— gave entrée to night spots and supper clubs where cocktails abounded. The drinks, savored in secret, could be all the more delectable if the cocktail shaker went "underground." The folly of Prohibition was bluntly exposed in a listing published in the *New York Telegram* in 1928 of the places where Americans could imbibe and/or obtain alcoholic beverages, which included:

> restaurants, night clubs, bars behind a peep-hole, dancing academies, delicatessens, drug stores, cigar stores, confectioneries, soda fountains, behind partitions of shoe-shine parlors, back rooms of barbershops, from hotel bellhops, from hotel day clerks, night clerks, in express offices, in motorcycle delivery agencies, paint stores, malt shops, cider stubes, fruit stands, vegetable markets, taxi drivers, groceries, smoke shops, athletic clubs, grill rooms, taverns, chophouses, importing firms, tea rooms, moving-van companies, spaghetti houses, boarding-houses, Republican clubs, Democratic clubs, laundries, social clubs, newspaper-men's associations.

In addition, a new social event—the elaborate cocktail party staged in a private home—emerged in these years, and women eagerly took part, smashing the gender barrier that had long forbidden "ladies" from entering into the gentlemen-only barrooms and cafés. A Jazz Age flapper, seemingly plucked from the pages of a novel by F. Scott Fitzgerald, could put her high-heeled foot on the brass rail and order herself a drink in whatever nighttime hideaway club or lounge was the fashion of the moment.

Even as cocktail recipes from the pre-Volstead years circulated in dog-eared bartenders' guides, such as Harry Johnson's *Bartender's Manual* (1882) or William (Bill) Boothby's *American Bartender* (1901), mixologists of the twenties owed much to the titans of the preceding generation. The debut of the American cocktail in the Gilded Age saw Johnny Solon conjure the Bronx cocktail at the Waldorf-Astoria Hotel bar, while Henry C. Ramos delighted scores with his Ramos Gin Fizz at Meyer's Hotel Internationale restaurant in New Orleans. The greatest maestro of them all was (and is to this day) "Professor" Jerry Thomas (b. 1830), who tended bar on both US coasts as well as in St. Louis and London. His pioneering *Bar-tender's Guide* (1862), introducing ten classic cocktails, followed by *The Bon-Vivant's Companion* (1877), featuring 130 drinks "in endless variety," were virtual Baedeker guides to the world of spirits.

The fundamental ingredient that Thomas and his Gilded Age cohorts bequeathed to the Roaring Twenties bar was, quite simply, ice, which had long been cut from frozen lakes and rivers, crucial for preserving perishables, before its manufacture in ice plants in the 1870s. No one knows who first slipped a few chips or chunks of ice into a straight whiskey or gin drink, but the "dilution" proved revolutionary. The imbiber's fear that the beverage had been cheapened promptly yielded to the pleasure of a cool drink enhanced by its visual appeal in tall clear glassware. *Eureka!* The modern cocktail was born and the original Manhattan, Old Fashioned, and Martini soon got a Roaring Twenties twist as the decade produced its own distinctive cocktail menu.

The giddy imbibers drank, in part, to stave off the hangover induced by catastrophic events of the prior decade that cast long shadows on Jazz Age culture and helped define it. The First World War—a bloody international conflagration that from 1914 to 1918 left some twenty million soldiers and civilians dead—made itself felt in the stories and novels of iconic writers of the 1920s such as F. Scott Fitzgerald, Ernest Hemingway, and John Dos Passos, with their vivid scenes of warfare, injury, and lifelong trauma. In Fitzgerald's novel *Tender Is the Night* (1934), set in the French Riviera, the lead character, a physician, points to a little stream, a two-minute walk from bank to bank. He muses, "It took the British a month to walk to it—a whole empire walking very slowly, dying in front and pushing forward behind. And another empire walked very slowly backward a few inches a day, leaving the dead. . . . No Europeans will ever do that again in this generation." "All my beautiful lovely safe world blew itself up here," he reflects.

Claiming even more victims than the war, the influenza pandemic of 1918 had also left the world reeling. Thought to have been first detected at Fort Riley, a Kansas army base, in March 1918, the misnamed Spanish flu (H1N1 virus) took tens of millions of lives worldwide over the next eighteen months and left many impaired. President Woodrow Wilson, an ardent supporter of US participation in the war, downplayed the severity of the devastating flu, and reports of its transmission were widely suppressed. According to historian John M. Barry, "It came in masquerade . . . then pulled down its mask and showed its fleshless bone."

Years later, two Parisian bars brazenly offered their patrons a liquid reminder. Harry MacElhone, a Scot, put a recipe for the "Flu," served at the Paris watering hole he bought and renamed Harry's New York

Bar, in his *ABC of Mixing Cocktails* (1930), while the Italian Piero Grandi included the "Flu," a concoction of whiskey, ginger brandy, lemon juice, sugar syrup, and Jamaica ginger bitters served at his bar at the Paris Ritz, in *Cocktails* (1920–27). In a farewell gesture to the pandemic's ending, London's Savoy Hotel bar offered the decades-old Corpse Reviver, a cognac and sweet vermouth blend mixed by Harry Craddock, the American "expat" bartender who decamped to the Savoy when Prohibition struck. By 1920, the one million Americans who had donned surgical masks for the duration had eagerly cast them aside and put the flu behind them.

A post-WWI Red Scare likewise kept the nation on edge. The country's wartime fury at all things German (sauerkraut shunned, Beethoven banned in Boston) morphed into a postwar terror that Bolshevism was taking root on US soil. The 1917–23 Russian Revolution that eventually installed Bolshevik rule under Vladimir Lenin had stirred Americans' fears that a radical minority of anarchist or communist immigrants could ignite full-blown revolution at home. The US Espionage Act and Sedition Act of 1917–18 alerted the public that treason was afoot, and the discovery of forty bombs addressed to prominent Americans and ready for postal delivery heightened the terror in 1919. That year, the US attorney general, A. Mitchell Palmer, launched nighttime assaults on American citizens that led to arrests and deportations, but the infamous Palmer Raids, later termed a government "witch hunt," failed to advance the attorney general's presidential ambitions, and the Red Scare petered out.

The world of sports had suffered its own crisis. Though the "Black Sox" bribery scandal of 1919, in which eight Chicago White Sox players were accused of throwing the World Series, left no legacy of libation, a cocktail was to be named for Arnold Rothstein, the gangster who "fixed" the series (Rothstein's exploits filled a criminal atlas well beyond the baseball diamond). A flurry of other scandals soon entered the

American lexicon: bribery surrounding the awarding of leases on oil reserves at Teapot Dome reached into the Harding administration; the racist nativism of the Ku Klux Klan was on the rise and exploded in a series of race riots during the "Red Summer" of 1919; the drama of the so-called "Monkey Trial" played out in the summer of 1925 in a courtroom in Dayton, Tennessee, when two celebrated attorneys, Clarence Darrow and William Jennings Bryan, debated the merits of evolutionary science against organized religion; while in Massachusetts anti-immigrant frenzy rushed Italian laborers Nicola Sacco and Bartolomeo Vanzetti through a hasty trial for murder and sent them to the electric chair.

Through it all, Americans drank, and a panoply of cocktails commemorate the era. The Dance the Charleston honored the latest ballroom fad, while the Mary Pickford nodded to the beloved star of the silver screen. The rocketing stock market, together with Florida's 1920s land boom, inspired the Millionaire, and baseball's Babe Ruth was toasted with the Sultan of Swat. The danger of the illicit liquor trade was memorialized in the Original Gangster, the St. Valentine's Day Massacre, the Tommy Gun, and others. Crime rose, fortunes were amassed, and a slew of new cocktails were shaken, stirred, and poured in hideaways to brand the "roaring" 1920s, according to one wit, the era of "Alcohol and Al Capone."

Alas, the zeal of temperance activists was short-lived. In the spring of 1933, Congress proposed a repeal of Prohibition, receiving enough support from the states for the Twenty-First Amendment to be ratified by December, putting a swift end to a period of American history that pundit H. L. Mencken dubbed "the thirteen awful years."

THE COCKTAIL HOUR

ocktails! Never was the cherished word so endangered as on January 16, 1920, when the detested Volstead Act became law and launched the puritanical reign of Prohibition. A spirited rebellion began. From that day forward, "cocktail" would be spoken in defiance, whether murmured softly and seductively, or broadcast boldly and brashly. The year, 1920, and the rascal in whose name the dreadful law had passed would be toasted so far away as the cocktail hour at Harry's New York Bar in Paris, where the Volstead Cocktail and the Nineteen-Twenty Cocktail tempted thirsty Americans.

In the US, the social observer Gilbert Seldes's account *The Future of Drinking* (1930) hailed Prohibition's "new drinks, new ways of drinking," and the bemused Seldes imagined cocktail disputes flaring in apartments, speakeasies, suburban homes, and wherever else the cocktail shaker's percussive maraca promised chilled libations. "No two mixers of cocktails to-day agree on ingredients or proportions," Seldes admitted, "or any of the recondite points of making and serving drinks."

The cocktail culture celebrated in the *Smart Set*, a magazine aimed at the most fashionable urbanites, cast the Martini, Manhattan, and Old Fashioned as a classic "holy trinity" of libations. Editor George Jean Nathan shuddered to list the "hundred and one ridiculous mixtures, without rhyme or reason," among them the new Chocolate cocktail and the Colonial, which "performed the atrocity of defiling its gin with grapefruit juice and maraschino." The Puritan, he continued, featured "acid phosphate, rye whiskey, and Calisaya" (an herbal liqueur). Otherwise, Nathan trembled to admit, "bourbon was contaminated with ginger ale" and "brandy was ignited to amuse the children." What's more, allegedly "ideal drinks" befouled inexperienced women's tastes with cocktails that "approached as closely as possible the ice-cream soda and the banana split" (Nathan's case in point: the Alexander). Men who served woman these drinks, the tart connoisseur of cocktails remarked, "tried so hard to suggest that drinking was aphrodisiac and so hard to forget that drinking, in any decent civilization, is an end in itself."

The indecency of the liquor itself drew Gilbert Seldes's sharpest censure. He blamed the bootlegger for "constantly committing a crime against drink, by adulteration." Americans, he regretted, had long sought liquor—"not so much drunk as swallowed"—for "pure kick," but Prohibition had resulted in "some of the foulest mixtures known to man," while "the actual taste of Scotch and gin began to vanish" amid concoctions of synthetic liquors. Fashion maven Diana Vreeland recalled, "It was because you weren't allowed to drink that you drank anything you could get your hands on. People would go into the bathroom and drink Listerine."

The electric refrigerator promised the extinction of the antediluvian ice box and faithful ice man. In truth, the tiny freezer compartments in the General Electric or Kelvinator fridge strained for hours to chill a few gridded trays of water to 32 degrees Fahrenheit and failed utterly to meet the demands of the cocktail hour. Nathan admonished all hosts and hostesses, for the sake of a properly chilled Martini or Manhattan or a sufficiently iced Old Fashioned, to abjure their kitchen refrigerators, call the ice house to order a fifty-pound bag of crystal-clear cubes, settle the bag in the sink, and rely on it to outlast the party, should the guests not depart until dawn.

Scenes of cocktail parties flourished in novels and short stories, mirroring the gatherings taking place nationwide during the supposedly "dry decade." In his novel *The Beautiful and Damned* (1922), F. Scott Fitzgerald's newlyweds receive as a wedding gift "an elaborate 'drinking set,' which included silver goblets, cocktail-shaker, and bottle-openers."

The Prohibition era, the novel insists, promoted "more drinking than ever before," for "one's host now brought out a bottle on the slightest pretext." A party is the pretext in Dorothy Parker's story "Big Blonde," which follows the sentimental, buxom Hazel Morse, who joins a neighbor's nightly parties where "The Boys" bring "plenty of liquor." Popular with "many men," while drinking, Hazel becomes "lively and good-natured and audacious." Though Hazel expresses the desire "that whisky would be her friend," readers see her life unravel under its influence.

Novelist John Dos Passos, like Parker, understood the terrible toll of alcoholism, but a cocktail party for two in *The Big Money* (1936) insures the bachelor host's sly scheme of seduction. Charley Anderson brings out a wicker tray with "the fixings for old fashioneds" and "a plate of sandwiches" to woo his fetching young female guest. Charley's New York bachelor pad window cinematically displays the setting winter sun, and several sandwiches and whiskey drinks measure the cocktail hour until, at the prime dusk-to-dark moment, "he got her to take her dress off."

Perhaps the author who best limned the cocktail scene was Sinclair Lewis, who became the first American to win the Nobel Prize for literature in 1930 for a series of novels that beamed a satirical searchlight on middle-class manners and mores in America's heartland. One of his best-known and bestselling works, *Babbitt* (1922), is set in the bustling city of Zenith in an unnamed Midwestern state, where George F. Babbitt, at forty-six years of age, counts himself an avid motorist, proud member of the Boosters Club, family man, and homeowner (as well as a realtor known to be "nimble in selling houses for more than people can afford to pay").

The novel mirrors the practices of the Prohibition era from the beginning, when Babbitt quaffs a friend's "tremendous home-brewed beer" and later downs "corrosive bootlegged whisky" in a convention hotel where, quite drunk, he is figuratively rendered "blind and deaf" (a nod to the actual lethal effects of tainted Prohibition alcohol). Babbitt's confab with a local Zenith patrician about church matters begins with a wintertime "whisky toddy" at his host's baronial home, where the fine liquor is truly aged and bottled in bond. Babbitt can barely restrain himself from bursting out, "Oh, maaaan, this hits me right where I live!" ("Nor had he, since prohibition, known anyone to be so casual about drinking.")

In another instance, in advance of a dinner party to be hosted by the Babbitts in their suburban Floral Heights home, George needs to procure gin. One possibility, the so-called "bathtub gin," would require a trip to the hardware store for a legal gallon of denatured alcohol, to which Babbitt would add distilled water, glycerine, and oil of juniper. Voilà, gin! The libation à la Babbitt would be bottled in kitchen glassware, perhaps Mason or Ball jars used for homemade preserves, although author Sinclair Lewis knew that his upright, self-respecting

Floral Heights citizen would be mortified to bootleg his own booze. So Babbitt visits the local bootlegger, where an overpriced quart of gin is sworn to be "the real stuff, smuggled from Canada."

Armed with the gin, Babbitt returns home. "Hey, Myra," he calls to his wife, "want a little nip before the folks come?" She declines, but Babbitt's taste "fills him with a whirling exhilaration" and the desire "to rush places in fast motors, to kiss girls, to sing, to be witty."

By evening, the host of Floral Heights welcomes his guests, who expect their "canonical rite" of a cocktail upon Babbitt's invocation, "Well, folks, do you think you could stand breaking the law a little?" As he moves "majestically" among his guests to mix the cocktails—one drink for the wives, two for the husbands—Babbitt feels as "authoritative" as a saloon bartender as he "chip[s] ice and squeeze[s] oranges," although he drew the line at a cocktail shaker, the "proof of dissipation, the symbol of a Drinker." His "ancient gravy-boat" and a pitcher minus its handle suffice to produce a "fine old cocktail" that tastes "kind of a Bronx, and yet like a Manhattan." At last, when the final drop of "the sacred essence" has left the pitcher, the men "stood and talked about prohibition."

THE BRONX

Ingredients

1. ⅔ ounce gin
2. ⅓ ounce orange juice
3. 1 dash French vermouth
4. 1 dash Italian vermouth
5. Ice cubes

Directions

1. Add 2–3 ice cubes to shaker.
2. Add gin and orange juice to shaker.
3. Add vermouth dashes.
4. Shake, strain, and serve.

MARTINI

Ingredients

1. 2¼ ounces gin
2. 2 teaspoons dry vermouth
3. 1 dash orange bitters
4. Brined olive or lemon peel twist for garnish

Directions

1. Put gin and vermouth into mixing glass.
2. Add ample ice, stir until fully chilled.
3. Strain into cocktail glass and add bitters and garnish.

MANHATTAN

Ingredients

1. 1½ ounces Canadian whisky
2. ½ ounce dry vermouth
3. 2 teaspoons sweet vermouth
4. 1 dash orange bitters
5. Maraschino cherry for garnish

Directions

1. Put first four ingredients into mixing glass.
2. Add ample ice and stir gently.
3. Strain into cocktail glass and garnish with cherry.

CHOCOLATE COCKTAIL

Ingredients

1. ½ ounce rye whiskey
2. 1½ ounces Bénédictine
3. 1 teaspoon cocoa powder
4. 1 egg white

Directions

1. Put all ingredients into shaker.
2. Add ample ice.
3. Shake very vigorously.
4. Strain into chilled cocktail glass.

COLONIAL COCKTAIL

Ingredients

1. 2 ounces dry gin
2. 1 ounce grapefruit juice
3. 2 teaspoons maraschino liqueur
4. Grapefruit peel twist

Directions

1. Put first three ingredients in shaker.
2. Add ample ice cubes.
3. Shake vigorously.
4. Strain into cocktail glass and garnish with twist.

ALEXANDER COCKTAIL

Ingredients

1. 1 ounce brandy or gin (your choice)
2. 1 ounce crème de cacao
3. 1 ounce heavy cream

Directions

1. Put chosen gin or brandy into shaker.
2. Add other ingredients.
3. Shake vigorously.
4. Strain into cocktail glass.

VOLSTEAD COCKTAIL

Ingredients

1. 1 ounce Canadian Club whisky
2. 1 ounce Swedish punsch
3. ½ ounce orange juice
4. ½ ounce strawberry syrup
5. 1 dash anisette

Directions

1. Put ingredients in mixing glass.
2. Add ample ice and stir gently.
3. Strain into cocktail glass and serve.

NINETEEN-TWENTY COCKTAIL

Ingredients

1. ½ ounce gin
2. ½ ounce kirschwasser
3. 1 ounce French vermouth
4. 1 teaspoon groseille (currant) syrup
5. 1 dash absinthe

Directions

1. Put ingredients into shaker.
2. Add ample ice and shake vigorously.
3. Strain and serve in cocktail glass.

CRIMINAL INTENT

You can't cure a thirst by law.

—Alphonse ("Al") Capone

Straight away, the "curative" powers of the Volstead Act became a national joke and a bonanza for entrepreneurs already skillful in racketeering, gambling, running bawdy houses, and other vices. To support the new law, pious "drys" held theatrical funerals for John Barleycorn, bidding "Goodbye" to "God's worst enemy" and "Hell's best friend." Meanwhile, a different law quietly took firm hold in the Prohibition years. Set forth in 1776 by a British economist, Adam Smith, the law of supply and demand governed the trade in spirited beverages and beer as bootleggers hustled to meet a thirst that burgeoned from US cities to hamlets. Smith's law allegedly operated by an "invisible hand," a metaphor the barons of booze could relish. Prohibition would reportedly decrease the number of "stick-up men, payroll robbers, jewelry thieves, burglars, and safe blowers" because the great majority had gone into "booze running," which paid so much better.

Suddenly, in this topsy-turvy new world, the traditional duties of legitimate brewers, distillers, retailers, and tavern keepers became crimes. The criminals, for their part, often fronted as legitimate businessmen—a florist, a dry cleaner, a warehouse operator, a cigar store proprietor. Imbibers in years to come often romanticized their bootleggers as rogue adventurers, each one a "bold spirit who ran rum and shot down hijackers and otherwise defied the government." The truth only dawned "when the genial drinkers became suddenly aware of the fact that the bootlegger was trafficking in liquor . . . for the money." With the Eighteenth Amendment, a schooner of beer that used to sell for a nickel or a shot of booze that went for a dime might now cost ten times as much.

The new day dawned within weeks of Prohibition's inauguration. Congress was informed that month that the wholesale smuggling of liquor was in progress on the borders and a mere infinitesimal quantity seized. In Brooklyn, carloads of patent medicine (at 55 percent alcohol) were seized, while an Illinois official "estimated that 300,000 spurious prescriptions had been issued by Chicago physicians since the law became effective." In Baltimore, federal Prohibition agents were arrested for corruption, as was a deputy collector of internal revenue in New York City. Citizens who were implored to surrender their home stills instead fired up their "alki-cookers." A still with a capacity of 130 gallons daily was found operating five miles north of Austin, Texas, on the farm of US senator Morris Sheppard, who had tweaked the Volstead Act and gained credit as an author of the Eighteenth Amendment. Prohibition cases quickly clogged the courts, and the future for bootleggers could not have been brighter.

Distillers and vintners, meanwhile, adapted as best they could. The Jack Daniel's distillery, acquired by a bootlegger, produced alcohol for legal "medicinal use," while vintners sold grape juice and "sacramental wines" to those who suddenly had "found religion." The Anheuser-Busch brewery sold yeast and beer-making kits for the home brewer while producing "near-beer," a watery beverage with minimal alcoholic content. Numerous breweries, vintners, and distilleries went bankrupt, their brands ghostly memories.

The Brooklyn-born Alphonse Capone (b. 1899), the son of Italian immigrants, would become the most successful of these businessmen, exploiting the vast space between the unquenchable demand for liquor and the limited supply. Capone had left school at age fourteen and worked briefly in a book bindery, a print shop, and an ammunition factory. The boyhood street gangs and "strong-arm terror" in his native Brooklyn and on the Lower East Side, however, made "the streets" his "apprenticeship," writes biographer Robert J. Schoenberg, who details Capone's schooling under New York mobster Frankie Yale (born Ioele) and especially John Torrio, the "thinking man's criminal." A diminutive figure who ruled by brain power, Torrio employed musclemen to do his bidding with a crook of his soft fingers. (His pacific slogan, "There's plenty for everyone," anticipated Capone's mantra, "We don't want any trouble.")

In 1918, in New York, he married the Irish Mae Coughlin and became the father of infant Albert Francis Capone. The previous year, he had learned a hard lesson in anger mismanagement when, working as a bartender and bouncer in Frankie Yale's dive, the Harvard Inn, Capone's customary finesse failed him and nearly cost him his life. The muscular Al, at five feet, ten inches tall, had insulted a patron's kid sister with a compliment about her "nice ass," whereupon he faced the avenging knife blade of her brother, who, fortunately for Capone, missed the jugular but slashed Al's left cheek. In years to come, when Capone ruled from Chicago, the nickname Scarface was uttered at one's peril.

In 1919, Al Capone ventured to Chicago as the lieutenant of his mentor Torrio. Primed for Prohibition and Capone, the city had earned its boomtown reputation for meatpacking, grain shipping, manufacturing, railroads—and colorful politicians who dispensed patronage and turned a blind eye to gambling, brothels, bribery, and various other vices, all carried out under lax policing. The Torrio plan, at the time, was to bolster a well-entrenched criminal ally with deep roots in Chicago politics and law enforcement and to expand routine criminal enterprises in a capacious city. With the Eighteenth Amendment, everything changed. To Capone, as to Torrio and others, the "new wrinkle of national prohibition . . . was an answered prayer."

The features of Prohibition-era law enforcement looked so favorable to Al Capone and other bootleggers that they might have conjured them up themselves. Throughout the "dry decade" and until the repeal of Prohibition, Washington, DC, would repeatedly shift the burden of enforcement to the states, and the states ping-ponged the burden back to the halls of Congress, which duly appropriated fractions of the money necessary for serious enforcement (little more than the $4.6 million appropriated in 1921). Penalties for transgression were paltry. A first offence called for a maximum one year in jail and a fine of $1,000, but "federal judges fined few the maximum and sent fewer to jail." Agents were paid a mere $35 per week (less than trash haulers), and a series of well-intentioned Prohibition Bureau chiefs would plunge from righteous zeal to burnout, complaining that local authorities and police thwarted their every move. By 1926, after six years of Prohibition, 875 agents of the enforcement service would be dismissed for such offences as bribery, extortion, solicitation of money, conspiracy to violate the law, embezzlement, and submission of false reports. By 1930, the Prohibition Bureau would announce plans "to train agents to act always as gentlemen, to use their brains rather than their brawn in discharging their duties." (Agents were to use weapons solely "for self-defense.") President Warren G. Harding was to warn that violations of the Prohibition Act "bred a contempt for law" that might "ultimately destroy the Republic," but neither he nor his successors, presidents Calvin Coolidge and Herbert Hoover, exerted executive authority for serious enforcement. Charles W. Eliot, president of Harvard University, declared that "people with money and social position were helping to defeat the law." "They are teaching lawlessness, especially to the young men of the country."

The young men's and women's favorite libations flowed freely because, from the beginning, Messrs. Al Capone, John Torrio, and others saw daylight through loopholes that eluded the Washington solons who had reasoned that, "once there were no wet states, there would be no problem, for there would be no liquor to defeat the law." One glaring loophole was liquor legalized for "medicinal purposes," and by July 1920, over "fifteen thousand physicians and fifty-seven thousand druggists and manufacturers of medicines and extracts had applied for licenses to prescribe and dispense intoxicating liquor." The twenty Walgreen Drug stores operating in 1919 expanded to 601 stores in thirty states in a decade. Next to the medicine bottle stood the beer tankard, since the law was kinked by the requirement that a brewery first produce beer with its usual full 3–4 percent alcoholic content, but then reduce the alcohol to one-half percent, or near-beer. Ironically, it became common practice to "needle" near-beer with alcohol to boost the percentage, though countless breweries evaded the law to produce robust beers for regular customers and those who could talk their way into a secret taproom whose outdoor sign might read "Sea Food."

In 1924, en route to the Republican national convention in Cleveland, thirsty journalist H. L. Mencken and book publisher Alfred Knopf were able to persuade local skeptics in Pennsylvania that they were not, as suspected, federal agents—Mencken used the German term for a beer schooner or mug: *Humpen*—and recalled, "Knopf had two, and I had three, and two sandwiches," all for "sixty-five cents." In Cleveland, where, he quipped "a glass of malt liquor was as hard to come by . . . as an honest politician," the journalist was tipped off that parched Cleveland would receive "ten cases of bottled beer and ale . . . sent down the Detroit River to Lake Erie," to be delivered at a Cleveland

breakwater on the Cuyahoga River. In Mencken's humorous account, the foiled delivery from Canada involved a rowboat and couriers who quaffed the brews, but he underscored the commonly acknowledged fact that Americans often relied on alcoholic beverages supplied by smuggling.

In historian Charles Merz's tabulation, "The total distance vulnerable to smuggling by land and sea . . . was approximately 18,700 miles." Operating in Detroit, a gateway from Canada, the notorious Purple Gang (also known as the Sugar House Gang), hijacked and bootlegged liquor across the national border. This band of Jewish operators committed the violent, lethal acts that became a hallmark of the trade. In midafternoons, the gang typically sent two dozen fast launches across the narrow Detroit River from Windsor, Ontario, loaded with Canadian whisky, French brandy, American rye, and Canadian ales. (If a Purple Gang launch was seized by one of the two US government boats patrolling the river, the gang would buy back its own boat àt the next government auction.) Huge fortunes rose from liquor smuggling from north of the US border, notably by Canada's Samuel Bronfman (b. 1889), who seized opportunities to supply Americans with their favorite alcoholic libations.

A flourishing post-WWI chemical industry had also produced a host of products, including industrial alcohol, known as "denatured alcohol," that became a boon to bootleggers. Clear, tasteless, potent, and legal, it could be colored and flavored to taste enough like gin, bourbon, scotch, rye, or other spirits to pass for the genuine article. A wily bootlegger equipped himself with counterfeit labels and seals, vials of flavorings (iodine, creosote, juniper oil), and familiar bottles, in-cluding the "pinched" scotch bottle, together with colorings from burnt sugar or caramel. Bottled, corked, labeled, and sealed, the product's final, authentic touch was a saltwater bath to fade the labels and thus suggest the sea water of the rum-runner's schooner that brought the expensive, bottled-in-bond gins and liquors from England, Ireland, or the Scottish Highlands. In 1920, the US production of denatured al-cohol had jumped from seven to twenty million gallons. Bottled to sell as "the real thing," the counterfeit booze could reap fortunes for canny businessmen like Alphonse Capone.

Bootleggers counted on large illegal stills to supplement the indus-trial alcohol they purchased on the open market. A commercial still representing an investment of $500 could produce from fifty to one hundred gallons of liquor daily. The Prohibition Bureau pointed out that this liquor could be produced at a cost of fifty cents a gallon and sold for three or four dollars a gallon at or near the place of manufacture. Often situated in remote locations in the woods or countryside, a still could pay for itself in a few days and, if seized, another would easily crop up in a new location. The home distillery also became a moneymaker, easily assembled from a wash boiler or steam cooker and coils of copper tubing available for a few dollars. (Sears, Roebuck & Co.'s wash boilers had been featured for sale since 1897 in the annual mail-order catalogue under "Complete Kitchen Furniture Assortment.")

Those with elementary reading skills could visit the local Carnegie Library and find it furnished with magazines and books with self-help directions for distilling alcohol. The US Government Bulletins, free upon request, provided instructions for home distilling. In 1900, the US Department of Agriculture's Bureau of Chemistry had published "The Composition of American Wines," and in 1906, came Farmer's Bulletin No. 269 ("Industrial Alcohol . . . Uses and Statistics"). In 1910, the Bureau of Chemistry published "Manufacture of Denatured Alcohol." That same year saw Farmer's Bulletin No. 410 roll from the government printing press with advice on the uses of damaged potatoes ("Potato Culls as a Source of Industrial Alcohol"). These and other how-to pamphlets encouraged the distillation of alcohol through a "waste not, want not" usage of peelings, skins, rinds, cores, seeds, and the flesh of bananas, apples, watermelon, oats, sorghum, and potatoes that would have made Ben Franklin proud. Household scraps or greengrocers' trash could become the distiller's friend, and so could sugar, used in the illicit manufacture of alcohol. The production of corn sugar increased from 152 million pounds in 1921 to 960 million pounds in 1929.

Home stills became Aladdin's lamp for families scraping by in tenement slums in US cities, and the "Genies of the Lamp" were Messrs. Capone, Yale, Arnold Rothstein, and others in the business of booze, for they took the sweat out of the sweatshops. No longer must a family—men, women, and children—earn mere pennies squinting in dismal lamplight into the wee hours sewing buttons or fur trim on garments to be collected by a contracted "sweater" working for a clothing manufacturer. No longer need the single mother of young children scrub other women's floors on hands and knees to put bread on the table, nor a "breadwinner" feed his large family by laboring from dawn to dark almost every day of the year, earning pitiful wages shoveling and hoisting with his arms, legs, and back.

The bootlegger became a godsend to the hard-pressed "tired" and "poor" who were welcomed to America in Emma Lazarus's poem "The New Colossus," which had been engraved at the base of the Statue of Liberty. These "aliens," as the federal government termed immigrant violators of Volstead, found themselves on a 1920s easy street they could not have imagined as immigrants toiling in America. The mythic streets paved with gold became, in reality, apartments bubbling with distilled dollars when a representative of Mr. Capone came calling with a proposition and metallic equipment. (Occasionally Mr. Capone himself—the families' godfather—came to inspect and wish a family well.)

From raids to sting operations, the federal initiatives limped along. Social gathering places became easy targets for raids—hotels, restaurants, amusement parks, pool rooms, cabarets, delicatessens, roadhouses that were supplied with liquor and beer by the Capone organization, the Purple Gang, Frankie Yale's network, or others. Once the flashy newspaper publicity died down, the raids were forgotten, and speakeasies, if padlocked, soon turned up elsewhere. In 1927, the *New York Times* reported, "Jurors will not convict in liquor cases."

The government's sting operations became ever more desperate. At the Bridge Whist Club, a government-sponsored New York speakeasy, patrons drank bootlegged liquor served by undercover federal agents who planned to bring bootlegging suppliers to justice. The Whist Club was shuttered when both "wet" and "dry" congressmen declared it a

"dangerous precedent." Another federal plan—to smuggle liquor across the Canadian border and "dispose" of it to bootleggers who would then be arrested and raided—likewise fell afoul of officials who feared that law enforcement would dishonor itself in a scheme of "flagrant treachery." In desperation, officials of the Department of the Treasury concocted a third plan: to "doctor industrial alcohol with deadly poisons." Those who died would be considered suicides who had broken the law. Hotly debated, the plan was denounced as a "fiendish" plot. (A fallback plan to tincture denatured alcohol with loathsome flavorings was set aside, since cravings for booze would doubtless win out when a quick shot "down the hatch" guaranteed a kick.)

Agent Eliot Ness was to live on in legend (and a TV series) as the somber, square-jawed federal scourge of criminals, the face of law enforcement while press photographs and motion pictures showed stone-faced "Feds" smashing cases of whiskey and barrels of beer to send suds and spirits gurgling down gutters and drains. In the mid-1920s, however, two of the most effective *agents provocateurs* were the unassuming duo Izzy Einstein and Moe Smith, who used a series of disguises to gain access to the bootleggers' haunts. Colorful accounts of their exploits lifted readers' spirits when they read of cases and barrels of whiskey seized in a garage, in churches, at a graveyard, in countless saloons-on-the-sly. Among Izzy's and Moe's disguises: milk driver, automobile cleaner, grave digger, motorman, stableman, iceman, vegetable vendor, and, on one occasion, a trombone player. Intriguing as they were, the versatile twosome exposed a federal government that found itself unable to stem the sources of production and pursued the supply in driblets.

The pathway to riches for Al Capone and others looked clear. Hadn't John Torrio said, "There's enough for everybody"? Capone's arrival in Chicago caused no stir when he opened a second-hand furniture store at 2220 South Wabash Avenue and began low-level work as a bouncer at a seedy downtown club, Four Deuces, where he would become the bartender, then manager. Just twenty at the time, Capone struck others as a much older man. For over a year, he familiarized himself with the city's gambling halls and brothels, and the visionary Torrio foresaw expanding bootlegging operations from Chicago to the suburbs and outlying districts and well beyond.

The groundwork was laid. One hitch remained: their Chicago partner in crime, Jim Colosimo, who had deep, longstanding connections in the city and might inconveniently crimp the Torrio-Capone grand plan of action. Torrio had come to Chicago to join forces, but the opportunities Prohibition afforded brought a new day. Plans changed. Alliances must shift. A favorable call to triggerman Frankie Yale in New York sealed a deal, and Prohibition warfare erupted on the morning of

May 11, 1920, when the body of James ("Big Jim") Colosimo was found face down on the floor of his café, "blood pooled at his head, his body sprawled . . . close to the door." The fatal shot behind the right ear would be recognizable as "gang stuff . . . a carefully considered finisher through the head."

The lavish funeral inaugurated gangsters' "Obsequies Chic," biographer Schoenberg's term for the aggregation of politicos who turned out in force, along with judges, entertainers, "luminaries of the Chicago Opera Company," and "gamblers, dive operators, pimps and whoremasters." Extravagant floral arrangements with the killers' RIP henceforth became a Prohibition funeral standard. Both Torrio and Capone had established alibis for the Colosimo killing when questioned by the police. ("Me kill Jim?" cried Torrio. "Jim and me were like brothers.")

Blood ties, sacred to Al Capone, put his business headquarters at the Hawthorne Hotel in Cicero, a forty-minute drive south of the city, but the purchase of a fifteen-room brick house at 7244 South Prairie Avenue in Chicago established his home, where wife Mae and Sonny (son Albert) lived with Al's widowed mother, his sister, Mafalda, brothers Frank and Ralph, and sometimes cousins Charles, Rocco, and Joseph Fischetti. (On one occasion, when police arrived at the home with questions, they found an aproned Al Capone stirring a pot of spaghetti sauce.)

In Cicero, the master of the "Capone Castle" had learned that holding onto power required curbing a volcanic temper and maintaining efficiency by bootlegging based on a *sistemazione* of gangs, a corporation of sorts, a cartel. Capone preferred "the outfit." Loyal hired guns and bodyguards went on the payroll, and so did emissaries who were authorized to transact business. Capone's trusted bookkeeper, Jack Guzick, tallied the orders for liquor smuggled and collected from stills and breweries. The bookkeeper kept track of the bodyguards' and drivers' weekly salaries of $100 to $500 and monitored the "balance sheets for brothels and gambling, the schedules for payoffs to politicians and police." Capone claimed he paid $30 million annually for political and police protection, while tens of millions of dollars flowed from the Capone rackets, brothels, casinos, liquor, and beer. For 1926 alone, US attorney Edwin Olson estimated Capone's gross income to be $70 million (in 1920s dollars).

With power came fame equal to Henry Ford's and Charles Lindbergh's. "When I sell liquor," Capone said, "it's called bootlegging. When my patrons serve it on silver trays, it's called hospitality." Always a dapper dresser, Capone ordered custom, top-of-the-line suits and shirts by the dozens in vibrant greens and yellows. When novelist Scott Fitzgerald conjured his fictional bootlegger in *The Great Gatsby*, he lingered on the "soft rich heap" of Gatsby's custom shirts "in coral and apple green and lavender and faint orange," surely a nod to the celebrity bootlegger. Known as "snorky," a current slang term for "stylish," in his inner circle Capone wore "wide-brimmed signature hats . . . the hue and texture of Grade A cream," and his pinkie finger gleamed with an 11.5-carat diamond ring. His motorcade on Chicago's streets attracted curbside crowds who recognized the Ford "flivver" in the lead, followed by a sedan filled with armed bodyguards, and, at last, the chauffeured armored Cadillac, a seven-ton, twenty-thousand-dollar fortress, thrice the weight and cost of showroom models. "There goes Al!" bystanders cried, and Capone "acknowledged the plaudits with a wave of his fat black wand of a cigar."

His generosity to strangers and racetrack gambling losses became legendary. Carrying a "$50,000 whip-out wad," Capone peeled off bills for hard-luck cases and hard-luck horses. The man had an unerring eye for losing racehorses that cost him millions of dollars. Unfazed, he wagered again and again—and cheerfully lost. His bets on those suffering life's misfortunes put him on the benefactor's winning side. "If people were desperate and needed help," one woman recalled, "he was there to help them. . . . He didn't expect anything in return." "Merchants in

Cicero had standing orders to give the needy coal, come winter, and groceries and clothes any time, charging Capone." When the crash came in 1929, "he was the first to open soup kitchens." "People thought of Capone," said a Cicero policeman, "as Robin Hood."

One "business expense," otherwise known as the cost in human lives, was mounting. Numerous mandatory "hits" factored in the inevitable turf battles, rivalries, and scores to be settled. In one instance, a Capone gunman, Jack McGurn, yearned to avenge his father's murder by henchmen of Frankie Yale. His father had been holding three nickels in hand at the moment of his death, and when Jack killed the three gunmen he thought had slain his father, he left one nickel in each corpse's palm. Other killings were not so personal. Rivals like the vicious Sicilian Gennas on the city's North Side, who refused to cooperate and menaced Capone's operation, were simply snuffed out. And a police raid sealed Charles Dean ("Deany") O'Banion's fate when the Irishman was pegged as a double-crosser in a beer deal. Hijacked beer trucks brought a hail of fatal bullets to Frankie Yale when he, too, double-crossed Al Capone.

The killings continued apace, at times when dynamiting with TNT accidentally cost lives which, many years hence, were to be termed "collateral damage," but especially when the portable Thompson machine gun, a military weapon, hit the city streets. Rounds fired from handguns often missed their targets, but the rapid-fire spray from a Tommy gun meant a gunman need only keep pressure on the trigger for "continuous, rapid-fire operation" of a weapon that fired one hundred rounds per minute. Its light weight, just over eight pounds, meant its user could carry more rounds and vastly improved homicidal efficiency.

The crescendo of killings was chronicled by Chicago *Herald-Examiner* reporter Edward D. Sullivan, who found that from the mid-1920s on over "seventy 'big shots' [were] killed in direct connection with booze, beer, gambling, and vice feuds in Chicago." Omitting the demise of "lesser lights," the reporter identified front-rank gangsters who were "killed in booze war," "killed in a roadhouse," "shot in saloon," "shot in front of home," "shot in his office," "killed in store." Many others were "taken for a ride" (driven "on rural rides from which there is no returning"). The outcome in every case: "slayer not caught."

On February 14, 1929, the violence culminated in the shocking "St. Valentine's Day Massacre," the resolution of a turf battle between Capone's South Side "outfit" and George Clarence ("Bugs") Moran's North Side Irish gang that shook a jaded Chicago to its marrow. The killers arrived at Moran's Lincoln Park garage in a police cruiser, four

of them dressed as policemen and thus readily admitted into the garage by Moran's men. Ordered to face the wall for what they assumed to be a routine police "frisk," the Moran gang complied and seven men were cut down in a hail of gunfire. (Al Capone, immediately suspected of the crime, was in Miami that day and made certain that his presence in south Florida was documented.)

Attempts on his life boosted Capone's celebrity, but the crime kingpin's fame infuriated authorities whose efforts to charge him with violent crimes had repeatedly failed. In the end, tax evasion became Capone's Achilles' heel, and in 1931 he was convicted on five counts and served nearly eight years in prison. His health suffered during and after imprisonment, and he died in January 1947, fourteen years after Prohibition ended.

CAPONE COCKTAIL

Ingredients

1. 2 ounces rye whiskey
2. 1 ounce Cointreau
3. ½ ounce fresh lemon juice

4. 1 teaspoon grated ginger

5. 3 slices orange

Directions

1. Muddle ginger, orange slices, and lemon juice in shaker.

2. Add rye and Cointreau.

3. Add ample ice and shake vigorously.

4. Strain into Old Fashioned glass with fresh ice.

ORIGINAL GANGSTER

Ingredients

1. 2 ounces bourbon whiskey

2. ½ ounce maraschino liqueur

3. ¾ ounce fresh lemon juice

4. Star anise for garnish

Directions

1. Put first three ingredients in mixing glass.

2. Add ample ice cubes and stir gently.

3. Strain into cocktail glass and garnish with anise.

DETROIT RIVER CROSSING

Ingredients

1. 2 ounces Canadian whisky

2. 2 teaspoons triple sec or curaçao

3. 2 dashes orange bitters

4. Twist of orange peel

Directions

1. In mixing glass, add first three ingredients.

2. Add ample ice cubes.

3. Stir gently.

4. Strain into cocktail glass.

5. Garnish with orange twist, first squeezing to release flavor.

TAKE THE NICKEL

Ingredients

1. 1 ounce white rum
2. 1 ounce Cocchi Americano
3. 1 ounce crème de pamplemousse rosé
4. 1 ounce fresh lime juice
5. Twist of lime peel

Directions

1. In mixing glass, add first four ingredients.
2. Add ample cubed ice.
3. Stir gently.
4. Strain into cocktail glass and garnish with lime twist.

TNT

Ingredients

1. 1 ounce Canadian whisky
2. 1 ounce absinthe
3. Star anise for garnish

Directions

1. Put whisky and absinthe into shaker.
2. Add ample ice and shake vigorously.
3. Strain into cocktail glass.
4. Garnish with anise and serve.

TOMMY GUN

Ingredients

1. ½ ounce dry gin
2. ½ ounce dark rum
3. ½ ounce white rum
4. ½ ounce cognac
5. ½ ounce Canadian whisky
6. ½ ounce scotch whisky
7. ½ ounce maraschino liqueur

8. 1 teaspoon lemon juice
9. 1 dash orange bitters
10. 3 ounces brut champagne
11. Orange slice

Directions

1. Put first ten ingredients into a shaker.
2. Add ample ice cubes and shake vigorously.
3. Strain into chilled glass and top with champagne.
4. Garnish with orange slice and serve.

SNORKY'S KISS

Ingredients

1. 1¼ ounces gin
2. ¾ ounce Byrrh
3. 1 teaspoon crème de cassis
4. Sprig of blackberry to garnish

Directions

1. Put first three ingredients into mixing glass.
2. Add ample ice and stir gently.
3. Strain into cocktail glass and add garnish.

ST. VALENTINE'S DAY MASSACRE

Ingredients

1. 1½ ounces scotch whisky
2. 1 ounce white rum
3. ½ ounce quince jelly
4. 3 ounces brut champagne
5. Twist of orange peel

Directions

1. Put first three ingredients into shaker.
2. Add ample ice and shake vigorously.
3. Strain into tall glass half-filled with crushed ice.
4. Top with champagne.
5. Stir very gently and garnish with orange twist.

TAX EVASION

Ingredients

1. I ounce scotch whisky
2. I ounce sloe gin
3. ¼ teaspoon absinthe
4. I dash Angostura bitters
5. Lemon peel twist to garnish

Directions

1. Put first four ingredients into Old Fashioned glass.
2. Fill with ice and stir gently.
3. Garnish with lemon twist.

BALLYHOO

THE MODERN MOMENT

Ballyhoo, noun (orig. U.S.). Trumped-up publicity of a
vulgar or misleading kind
—*Concise Oxford Dictionary of Current English*, 1929

As the decade took off, the seasoned newsman Silas Bent lamented the new tendency of the press to slight serious news to hype the ephemera of the moment, everything from prizefights to political fuss ("TUNNEY WINS CHAMPIONSHIP, BEATS DEMPSEY IN 10 ROUNDS"). He scorned the day's journalism as frivolous "ballyhoo" that lacked all gravitas, declaring, "The news is no bigger now, but the headlines are." No less ironic, then, that his scorching critique *Ballyhoo* (1927) gave the Roaring Twenties an embraceable word for an era that was happy to shorten its attention span to live in the moment.

"Ballyhoo" suited a generation that had bowed to the wartime ethos of "eat-drink-and-be-merry-for-tomorrow-we-may-die," then refused to resume the humdrum routine of the prewar world when it was over. "Their torn nerves craved the anodynes of speed, excitement, and passion," observed memoirist and historian Frederick Lewis Allen in *Only Yesterday* (1931). The traditional home, he said, had become "less of a shrine, more of a dormitory." Young women sought worldly jobs and independence, and Sigmund Freud and anthropologist Franz Boas taught that "men and women were merely animals of a rather intricate variety, and that moral codes . . . were often based on curious superstitions." A "spirit of revolt" by both sexes had made drinking "the thing to do." Four potent vials of the post-WWI revolution—Prohibition, the automobile, true confessions, and the movies—were poured into the Roaring Twenties cultural cocktail and fun and games ranged from crossword puzzles to sex in the back seat of a coupé. "Under the new regime, not only the drinks were mixed, but the company as well."

Titillation became the order of the day, and silly stunts welcome distractions. Goldfish swallowing became a fad (and inspired a cocktail), as did flagpole sitting. In 1926, Alvin ("Shipwreck") Kelly "put on a sitting" in Saint Louis, perched atop a pole for seven days and one hour, afterward touring other cities to break his own records. Newspapers publicized Kelly's exploits, just as they lent newsprint to the latest daredevil plunge over Niagara Falls on July 4, 1928, when Joseph ("Jean") Lussier forsook the usual wooden barrel in favor of a six-foot rubber ball lined with oxygen tubes. (Lussier survived and sold fragments of the shredded ball as souvenirs.)

Life-and-death extremes captured readers' attention. Grueling dance marathons were promoted as live entertainment, human endurance tests that forced couples to "dance" nonstop for hundreds of hours for prize money. (Dance marathoners risked collapse, and worse. In 1923, a young man died on the dance floor after trudging along with his partner for eighty-seven consecutive hours.) Two years later, another fatality played out publicly in Kentucky, when a spelunker, Floyd Collins, became trapped in a narrow crawlway in a cave fifty-five feet underground. For two weeks, rescuers maintained voice contact and supplied him with food and water as they tunneled downward, their progress blocked by a rock slide, until Collins succumbed to hunger,

thirst, and exposure. All the while, broadcast radio played its novel
part with bulletins, while newspaper publicity ballyhooed on a national
scale. Had the accident proved immediately fatal, remarked political
journalist Mark Sullivan, "the event would have received at most only
a paragraph or two in the local newspapers." As it was, "within a day
or two, Collins's name was on the first page of every newspaper in the
country." For a "vicarious" experience, insisted *Ballyhoo*, "the newspaper
undertakes profitably to provide the escape."

In word and deed, necking and petting preoccupied the younger
generation in the newly permissive postwar moment. "Petting and the

Campus," a 1925 *Survey* magazine article, reported on a Midwest student conference of college coeds at which seniors advised first-year girls about "how far to go" with boys, advising moderation lest girls "lose their heads." Those who went "too far" were "more fools than knaves," the sage seniors counseled, but one nagging question hung over the issue of social class: "Do 'nice' girls do it?" If they did, would their niceness be lost? The seniors linked sex to Prohibition: "Learn temperance in petting, not abstinence."

In college dorms and bedrooms, meanwhile, bodybuilder Bernarr Macfadden's magazine, *True Story*, tutored flappers-in-training about sex before marriage, adultery, and gateway kissing and temptation—and the horrid realization of consequences. Racy popular songs ("Hot Lips," "Burning Kisses") and novels amplified the magazine's stories, while Samuel Hopkins Adams's *Flaming Youth* (1923) portrayed young women in erotic arousal. Another such novel flummoxed reviewer Dorothy Parker, who admitted bafflement that a third-rate writer, Elinor Glyn, should top the bestseller list in 1927 with a book entitled, simply, *It*, a kind of Jazz Age *Fifty Shades of Gray*, though Parker acknowledged that the potboiler churned with scenes of gambling, opium, and lovers "vibrating away like steam launches." The impersonal pronoun "it" suddenly was uttered everywhere, meaning sexy, fashionable, first-rate, most likely to succeed. Mrs. Glyn "added meaning to the simple pronoun, 'it,'" remarked author Mark Sullivan, "transmuting that neutral little word into a noun and making it, for the younger generation . . . a symbol for the most desirable thing the gods could give." Movie actress Clara Bow became the "*It* Girl."

All along, the silver screen's exemplars of larger-than-life romance and its vicarious thrill tugged at flappers' heartstrings, none more so than Rudolph Valentino (Rodolfo Alfonso Raffaello Pierre Filiberto Guglielmi di Valentina d'Antonguella). Dubbed the "gigolo of every woman's dreams" in John Dos Passos's novel *The Big Money*, Valentino had made his mark in silent films, among others *The Four Horsemen of the Apocalypse, Blood and Sand*, and especially *The Sheik* and *The Son of the Sheik*. Now, press agents sprang into action when the thirty-one-year-old star suddenly succumbed to peritonitis in New York on August 23, 1926. "A posed picture of the funeral cortege was on the streets in one newspaper before the funeral cortege started," wrote one observer, and film star Mary Pickford was seen "sobbing bitterly as she followed the coffin from the actors' chapel" (St. Malachy's Roman Catholic Church). Stoked to "fever heat," mobs estimated at one hundred thousand persons stretched through eleven city blocks, storming the undertaker's business and smashing his plate glass window as scores were injured.

Valentino's body was taken west by train for a second funeral service in Beverly Hills, but public excitement waned with every state border the locomotive crossed. Dos Passos pronounced the Valentino ballyhoo to be over and done when he noted the news transiting from headlines to back pages: "The funeral train arrived in Hollywood on page 23 of the *New York Times*."

Tempus fugit, ballyhoo. . . .

GOLDFISH COCKTAIL

Ingredients

1. 1 ounce gin
2. 1 ounce Goldwasser
3. 1 ounce French vermouth

Directions

1. Put all ingredients in mixing glass.
2. Add ample ice and stir gently.
3. Strain into cocktail glass and serve.

VALENTINO

Ingredients

1. 2 ounces dry gin
2. 1 ounce Italian vermouth
3. ½ ounce Italian red bitter liqueur
4. Lemon twist (from peel)

Directions

1. In mixing glass, add first three ingredients.
2. Add ample ice and stir gently.
3. Strain into cocktail glass.
4. Garnish with lemon twist.

SHEIK HIGHBALL

Ingredients

1. 2 ounces dry gin
2. 1 ounce raspberry shrub
3. 3 ounces soda water
4. Lemon slice

Directions

1. Put gin and shrub in highball glass.
2. Add ample ice and stir gently.
3. Top with soda water.
4. Garnish with lemon slice.

PETTING PANTRY

Ingredients

1. 2 ounces gin
2. ¾ ounce passionfruit pulp
3. 2 teaspoons simple syrup
4. 1 teaspoon triple sec
5. 1 egg white

Directions

1. Put all ingredients into shaker.
2. Add ample ice.
3. Shake very vigorously.
4. Strain and serve in cocktail glass.

IT COCKTAIL

Ingredients

1. 1½ ounces dry gin
2. 1½ ounces Italian (sweet) vermouth
3. Orange bitters
4. Orange slice for garnish

Directions

1. Put first three ingredients into mixing glass with ice.
2. Stir gently but thoroughly.
3. Strain into ice-filled Old Fashioned glass.
4. Garnish with orange slice.

SOUL KISS

Ingredients

1. 1 ounce rye whiskey
2. 1 ounce French vermouth
3. ½ ounce Dubonnet
4. ½ ounce orange juice
5. Orange slice

Directions

1. Put first four ingredients in mixing glass with ice.
2. Mix well by gently stirring.
3. Strain and serve in cocktail glass.
4. Garnish with orange slice.

MAKING WHOOPEE

Ingredients

1. 1½ ounces Canadian whisky
2. ½ ounce dry vermouth
3. 1 teaspoon crème de cacao
4. 1 dash Angostura bitters
5. Piece of crystallized orange for garnish

Directions

1. Put first four ingredients into mixing glass.
2. Add ample ice and stir gently.
3. Strain into cocktail glass.
4. Garnish with orange piece.

NEWEST NEW WOMAN

With the Great War and the Spanish flu dispatched to the "dustbin of history" by cynical amnesiacs eager to move on, the 1920s "flapper" hatched like a new species, ready to stifle palaver about the good old days. Mark Sullivan, a chronicler of the times, found that 1922 marked "a distinct change for the worse . . . in feminine dress, dancing, manners, and general moral standards." Now, a young woman in her late teens or early twenties took the stage to shorten her skirts, roll her stockings, smoke cigarettes, drink gin, and pass her nights in smoky jazz clubs where she danced in "shockingly immodest fashion with a revolving cast of male suiters." Zelda Fitzgerald (b. 1900), flapper *par excellence* and chronicler of the species, said this new woman "bobbed her hair, put on her choicest pair of earrings and a great deal of audacity and rouge, and went into battle." Some feared that her fight was already won, that flappers had upended "the dear old fireside of long ago," as one newspaper editorial proclaimed, by inciting "all divorces, crime waves, high prices, unjust taxes, violations of the Volstead Act,

and crimes in Hollywood." The origin of the word "flapper" remained something of a mystery. Some thought the word mimicked loose galoshes flapping about young women's ankles. However cloudy the etymology, the flapper split the world into two camps in the early 1920s: those fearful of the new vixen, and those trying to make the best of her.

With F. Scott Fitzgerald, Zelda had married what one newspaper called the "flapper King," making her the Queen. (The couple were often androgynously fused as one, dubbed "The Fitz.") In the age of electrification, "The Fitz" were "live wires." Her husband had titled a story collection *Flappers and Philosophers* (1920), and Zelda prized his fictional women for the traits she saw in herself: "their courage, their recklessness and spendthriftness." The flappers' time-honored dismissal of elders' views gained special urgency in the fast-paced era of automobiles, movies, jazz, and the dance craze called the Charleston that was "prancing into favor," according to the *New York Times*. Zelda summed up the elders' era in a word—boring—adding that the flapper had succeeded the debutante. "The flapper flirted," Zelda declared, "because it was fun to flirt and . . . covered her face with powder and paint because she refused go through life with a deathbed air . . . or martyr-resignation."

Zelda may as well have been describing her own mother, Minnie Machen Sayre, who headed a nine-member household, including five children (one son, four daughters), in Montgomery, Alabama, where she was known to be "a little odd, or 'artistic'" but also the proper "stately and matronly" churchgoing wife of Judge Anthony D. Sayer. In short, a late-Victorian matron. But while Minnie indulged Zelda, her last-born child, elsewhere around the country, her maternal cohorts grumbled about daughters who had apparently landed from another planet. The girls were no longer "modest"; they dressed "differently" and were "bolder than they used to be." "Girls have more nerve nowadays—look at their clothes!" "Girls are more aggressive today. They call the boys up and try to make dates with them." The flappers also broke the barrier of class. The rouged girl of the past had been considered a slut from the "wrong" side of the tracks, but cosmetics now appeared on dressing tables previously set solely with a hairbrush, pins, and cold cream. "When I was a girl," lamented one mother, "a girl who painted was a bad girl—but now look at the daughters of the best families." Such plaints, recorded in *Middletown* (1929), the classic study of Muncie, Indiana, written by the husband and wife team of sociologists Robert Staughton Lynd and Helen Merrell Lynd, swirled amid similar apprehensions about the new, restless age.

The novelist Sinclair Lewis provided his own sharp assessment of youth, having explored numerous midsized American cities while doing research for *Babbitt* (1922), his fictional portrait of the life and times of the contemporary bourgeoisie. In 1921, Lewis spent two months in Ohio, Illinois, Wisconsin, and Michigan taking notes on the folkways of the US heartland. The fieldwork paid off when Lewis described an evening party in which Babbitt's son, a high school senior, entertains his friends at the family home. The forty-something Babbitt and his wife recall their youthful parties of charades and word games, but "these children seemed bold . . . and cold," the girls' lips "carmined and their eyebrows penciled." Word had spread about "'goings on' at young parties . . . of 'cuddling' and 'petting.'" The girls danced "cheek to cheek with the boys," and inside the cars parked at the curb Babbitt saw "points of light from cigarettes" and heard "giggles." He offered "dandy" ginger ale to the young men and felt like the "butler" when politely rebuffed. Young Ted Babbitt and his friends had dressed for the party with slicked-back "patent leather hair, wrinkled socks, and bell-bottom trousers," the mode that illustrator John Held, Jr., adapted for Scott Fitzgerald's *Tales of the Jazz Age* (1922). A shocked Babbitt "twice caught the reek of prohibition-time whisky," including the whiff on his son's breath. Mrs. Babbitt sighed in surrender. "All the mothers tell me," she says, "if you get angry because they go out to their cars to have a drink, they won't come to your house any more, and we wouldn't want Ted left out of things, would we?" (Babbitt hastens to be polite, lest son Ted be left out of things.)

The Babbitts youthful party guests, typical 1920s flappers and dudes, rejected kinship with a parental generation that cherished charades, housekeeping, and home-cooked family meals. Ted Babbitt's older sister, Verona, a stiff-necked graduate of Bryn Mawr College, shows no interest in domestic arts. In time, Mrs. Babbitt would surely feel as predictably horrified as was Zelda's mother at the sight of her daughter's slovenly household and indifference to the kitchen. (Invited to contribute to the volume *Favorite Recipes of Famous Women* [1925], Zelda

Fitzgerald offered the following breakfast advice: "See if there is any bacon, and if there is, ask the cook which pan to fry it in. Then ask if there are any eggs, and if so, try to persuade the cook to poach two of them. It is better not to attempt toast as it burns very easily. Also in the case of bacon, do not turn the fire too high, or you will have to get out of the house for a week. Serve preferably on china plates, though gold or wood will do if handy.")

Seen in history's rearview mirror, the flapper appears to have taken a detour from the Victorian family tree (agreeing with Henry Ford's dismissal of history as "bunk"), but the flapper descended directly from the "New Woman" who had jolted the country at the turn of the century and raised the curtain for her Roaring Twenties daughter. In

1898, popular humorist Finlay Peter Dunne created "Molly," the "new woman" who sorely tested her husband by riding a bicycle, demanding to vote, and "wearin' clothes that no lady should wear." Linking marriage with shackles, Molly proclaims that henceforth, "she'll be no man's slave."

The humorist hit a nerve. As far back as 1848 in Seneca Falls, New York, Elizabeth Cady Stanton had argued before a convention of feminists that marriage was a form of bondage—for a woman. Wedding vows meant the forfeiture of rights supposedly guaranteed in the US Constitution, and "I do" at the altar sounded like a coffin lid closing. Said Stanton, "in the eye of the law" a married woman was "civilly dead."

Stanton's words echoed into the next half-century, when a blockbuster novel, *The Awakening* (1899), flayed marriage as a trap and brought down a critical storm on its author, Kate Chopin (b. 1850). A New Orleans widow and mother of six, Chopin had published short stories in prestigious magazines (the *Atlantic*, *Vogue*) before daring to pen the novel that exposed "marriages that masquerade as the decrees of Fate." Aligned with a fictional young woman who could be her avatar, Chopin satirized "the women who idolized their children, worshipped their husbands, and esteemed it a holy privilege to efface themselves as individuals and grow wings as ministering angels." The young matron in *The Awakening* awakens sexually in an affair with a younger man, though the novelist bowed to the literary requirement that errant women must die, and so she was sent swimming into the sea to drown. Readers were not appeased, and Chopin's iconoclasm proved costly. Copies of the novel were torched, and the author found herself ostracized in New Orleans and her native St. Louis.

Vistas opened, nonetheless, for the American "maiden lady" with gumption. A leading light in the fight for Prohibition, Miss Frances E. Willard, president of the nationally prestigious Women's Christian Temperance Union, published a motivational miscellany for contemporaries of Mr. Dunne's "new woman." Willard's *Occupations for Women* (1897) chronicled scores of livelihoods available for ambitious women determined to escape what she termed "destiny's fierce crucible." American women in all walks of life testified in *Occupations for Women* that livelihoods awaited women lawyers, beekeepers, doctors, farmers, teachers, hairdressers, piano tuners, bankers, engineers, dressmakers, and on and on. The message in Willard's opus: fulfilling and financially nurturing careers beckoned, but only for those who avoided the trap of marriage. (Unless a woman was widowed, single parenting guaranteed social opprobrium.)

Willard included a chapter on "The Dramatic Profession" in her volume, but none could compare to a world-famous dancer and sexually liberated New Woman who by the Roaring Twenties was a legend. The San Francisco–born Isadora Duncan (b. 1877[?]) had triumphed through the 1910s on stages in France, Germany, and Italy, dancing barefoot while swathed in diaphanous costumes, and had performed with maestro Walter Damrosch's orchestra at New York's Metropolitan Opera House. She said of her art, "I followed my fantasy and improvised . . . any pretty thing that came into my head . . . a perfect pagan to all." (President Theodore Roosevelt attended one matinée, applauded vigorously, and told a friend that Isadora's dances reminded him of "a child dancing though the garden in the morning sunshine and picking the beautiful flowers of her fantasy.") "How beautiful the naked human body when inspired by beautiful thoughts," Isadora rhapsodized. "Dancing," she said, "is the Dionysian ecstasy."

Duncan's series of lovers evoked ecstatic memorial descriptions in her autobiography, published in 1927 just at the time she died in a freak accident, choking when the flowing neck scarf she wore in an open car tangled in the hubcaps. Reviewing the book for the *New Yorker*, the often-acerbic Dorothy Parker pulled out all the stops: "Please read

Isadora Duncan's *My Life*," Parker pleaded. "Here was a great woman, a magnificent, generous, gallant, reckless fated fool of a woman. . . . She ran ahead, where there were no paths."

For the Roaring Twenties flappers, Isadora's pages offered a model of new womanhood without marriage. *My Life* detailed romances aplenty but paused for a particular cautionary tale. One of Duncan's lovers, an ultrawealthy English yachtsman whom she tactfully called "L," "took it into his head that we should get married," though Isadora flatly opposed wedlock. She would be touring, she said, and what would he do all the while?

"L" replied that she would no longer need to tour. The dialogue as she remembered it:

"Then what should we do?"
"We should spend our time at my house in London, or at my place in the country."
"And then what should we do?"
"Then there is the yacht."
"But then what should we do?"

"L" proposed a three-month trial period. "And if you don't like it," he said, "I shall be much astonished."

To his Devonshire château in the countryside they went, and a succession of rainy days passed, each one exactly like another from breakfast through lunch, afternoon bridge games, dressing for dinner, until: "In the course of a couple of weeks," Isadora recalled, "I was positively desperate." Boredom had struck, the same ennui that afflicted Zelda Fitzgerald and her flapper cohorts, lined up in short skirts with arms bared to dance the "fast-stepping, toe-twisting, arm-swinging" Charleston. Flappers danced on the parapets of high-rise buildings, flew airplanes, drank cocktails. To dance was to be alive!

By chance, Isadora Duncan and the Fitzgeralds crossed paths in 1925 during dinner at an inn near Nice, France. Learning who was seated nearby, Scott "went to her table and sat at her feet." With her red dress and hair almost a match, and having grown somewhat heavy in her mid-forties, she was, nevertheless, the one and only Isadora Duncan. "She ran her fingers through Scott's hair and called him her centurion."

Zelda summed up the flapper's credo: "I refer to the right to experiment . . . as a transient, poignant figure who will be dead tomorrow." Sadly, both the King and Queen would die young, Fitzgerald in 1940 at age forty-four in Hollywood of a heart attack after a lifetime of alcoholism, Zelda seven years later at age forty-seven in a fire that consumed the hospital where she was awaiting electroshock therapy. "Flapperdom," she had written at an earlier time, "is making the youth of the country . . . intelligent and teaching them to capitalize their natural resources and get their money's worth."

THE FLAPPER COCKTAIL

Ingredients

1. 1½ ounces Jamaican rum
2. 1½ ounces French vermouth
3. 2 dashes Angostura bitters
4. Simple syrup (as desired)
5. Maraschino cherry
6. Orange slice

Directions

1. In mixing glass with ice, add rum, vermouth, and bitters.
2. Sweeten to taste.
3. Stir vigorously.
4. Put maraschino cherry in cocktail glass.
5. Strain and pour into cocktail glass.
6. Garnish with orange slice.

DANCE THE CHARLESTON COCKTAIL

Ingredients

1. 1¾ ounces Tom gin
2. 1 ounce Italian vermouth
3. 1 teaspoon orange marmalade
4. Orange peel twist

Directions

1. In cocktail shaker with ice, add gin, vermouth, and marmalade.
2. Shake vigorously.
3. Strain into six-ounce (Old Fashioned) glass with ice cubes.
4. Squeeze orange peel and add as garnish.

LIVE WIRE COCKTAIL

Ingredients

1. 1 ounce absinthe
2. 1 ounce green crème de menthe
3. Champagne (brut)
4. Star anise (for garnish)
5. Mint leaf (for garnish)

Directions

1. In mixing glass, add absinthe and crème de menthe.
2. Add ice.
3. Stir gently until quite cold.
4. Strain into champagne glass.
5. Slowly add champagne.
6. Gently but quickly mix and add garnishes.

ALL THAT JAZZ

The Jazz Age sound soared like a trumpet and wailed like a tenor sax as it drifted until dawn through the speakeasies, supper clubs, and dance floors of New York's jazz capital, Harlem. "A trip to Harlem has become the obligatory end of all good parties," insisted Prohibition's arbiter of culture, Gilbert Seldes, who perhaps recalled his wee hours at the Cotton Club, soaked in Sidecars, while listening to Duke Ellington's latest, "Mood Indigo." "If you have to ask what jazz is," quipped vocalist and trumpeter, Louis ("Satchmo") Armstrong, "you'll never know."

"Jazz" wended its way from "jasm," in fifty-year-old slang, meaning "spirit, energy, and pep." Updated for the twenties, it also became a verb, to "jazz it up," injecting speed and excitement into modern life. In 1925, journalist J. A. Rogers announced in *Survey* magazine that the term "jazz" overtopped the music itself to become "a spirit that can express itself in almost anything . . . a joyous revolt from convention, custom, authority, boredom, even sorrow—from everything that would confine the soul . . . and hinder its riding free on the air." "Jazz," Duke Ellington

would remark, "is the only unhampered, unhindered expression of complete freedom yet produced in this country."

Though the worldwide "elementals" of jazz preexisted in "the Indian war-dance, the Highland fling, the Irish jig, the Cossack dance . . . the hula of the South Seas," its immediate predecessor, he asserted, "is ragtime," a "direct descendent" of West African and Haitian music. The "faster and more complex" jazz tempo, Rogers added, bears "the marks of a nerve-strung, strident, mechanized civilization." Jazz in the twenties, he continued, ranks with "the movies and the dollar" as quintessentially American. Jazz orchestra leader Paul Whiteman defined jazz as "the folk-music of the machine age."

Fretful critics feared the explosive power of the syncopated, improvising newcomer to the musical scene. Social observer Mark Sullivan ruminated about "the insidious and conquering pervasiveness of the bizarre cacophony," while others dreaded that cherished musical genres, threatened by jazz, might become its victims. The Italian composer Pietro Mascagni declared that jazz had sounded opera's "death knell"; one English critic decried it as "musical insanity." In 1928, John Philip Sousa, the "American March King," declared that jazz didn't "truly represent America" and would "some day disappear."

Denizens of New Orleans, Chicago, and Kansas City fiercely claimed jazz as their birthright, but these geographic incubators sent vocalists, drummers, woodwinds, horns, and keyboard wizards to Harlem, the onetime Dutch colonial outpost that had become Prohibition's capital of nightlife. The area had housed first- and second-generation Irish who moved northward in the city after WWI, when an ambitious Black realtor, Philip A. Payton, promoted apartment rentals to Black tenants in buildings between 130th and 140th Streets from Fifth to Eighth Avenues, according to historian Jervis Anderson. "When the war brought waves of southern Negroes to find employment in the cities," Black Harlem spread further with "churches and cabarets," while "white patrons followed." Seventh Avenue became Black Broadway, "sleek and spacious, and well-groomed all day," and, "from five in the afternoon until after midnight, brilliant and glamorous and exciting as well." "You dressed if you went to Harlem," recalled Diana Vreeland, the legendary editor of *Vogue*, who spent numerous nights in its clubs.

Harlem's clubs blossomed when New York's fine-dining scene became a casualty of Prohibition. The bootleggers stepped in, gangsters like Owney Madden who issued orders from his Sing Sing prison cell, where he was serving a sentence for manslaughter, and Arnold Rothstein, who owned "pieces" of Harlem clubs and financed others. Funding the clubs and stocking the speakeasies, bootleggers made it "safe for people in 'ermine and pearls' to go uptown for entertainment and atmosphere . . . a few drapes, some silk splashed on the walls, and a tentlike effect over the dancefloor . . . a velvet rope, society people in the audience." The successful "club" was "full of booths and alcoves and cozy wall benches, which somehow contributed to the atmosphere of 'just us members,'" remarked chronicler Mark Sullivan.

The roughly five hundred Harlem speakeasies dovetailed with more established clubs along Seventh and Lenox Avenues—Club Hot Cha, Small's Paradise, Log Cabin, Theatrical Grill, Connie's Inn, Savoy Ballroom—and the legendary Cotton Club, where Cab Calloway's band alternated gigs with Duke Ellington's orchestra. In its earlier incarnations as the Douglas Casino (1918) and the Club Deluxe (1920), the venue had hosted banquets, dances, and private-party rentals, but in 1923, it reopened as the Cotton Club, with new theatrical jungle décor, a proscenium stage, dance floor, and seating for seven hundred. By one account, "all the performers were Black, but the club enforced a whites-only policy for customers and a $2.50 cover charge to keep out the undeserving poor. The shows were slickly professional and the service impeccable."

Jazz royalty routinely played Harlem. Trumpeter and vocalist Louis Armstrong (b. 1900) had been introduced to music as a street urchin confined to the Coloured Waifs' Home in New Orleans, where he learned the basics from his tutor, cornetist King Oliver, and later developed his signature "broad tone, smooth vibrato, and amazing virtuosity in the highest register" of the trumpet. Chicago became his musical bailiwick for much of the 1920s, but Louis Armstrong and His Stompers took up residence at Harlem's Connie's Inn in 1929.

At the Cotton Club, renowned as the "Aristocrat" of Harlem nightlife spots, Cab Calloway (Cabell Calloway III, b. 1907) danced,

conducted, and scatted his rendition of "Minnie the Moocher." His band alternated with Duke Ellington's eleven-member orchestra, attired in satin-trimmed beige tails, setting off their bandleader's elegant white suit as he conducted from the keyboard. Edward Kennedy Ellington (b. 1899), had garnered the nickname "Duke" as a well-dressed schoolboy who took piano lessons from the age of six in Washington, DC. The name stuck when he organized ensembles in his late teens, and, at age twenty-one, performed professionally with his group, Duke's Washingtonians. In New York by 1927, Duke Ellington and the Kentucky Club Orchestra soon shed its bourbon-tinged name to become Duke Ellington's Cotton Club Orchestra. At Ellington's insistence, Black patrons were admitted to the Cotton Club, although the audience remained predominately white, and the entertainment was designed to cater to its tastes.

Throughout the 1920s, a night at a Harlem jazz club was a necessary experience for any aspiring socialite as privileged partygoers sipped their cocktails while musical genius was displayed nightly from the bandstand. For thousands of others, the wickedly smart young columnist Lois Long, writing under the pseudonym Lipstick for the *New Yorker*, an upstart magazine of humor, culture, and opinion, provided a running commentary on the flapper lifestyle. Brash, energetic, and armed with a wicked sense of humor, Lois smoked, drank, and stayed up all night, then crashed in her office to recount the evening's adventures in her seemingly offhand magazine diary: "The gang would spill up to Harlem," she recounted. "Your first impression is of very pleasing decoration. The second impression is of a grand blues orchestra. And the third is probably the most inferior collection of white people you can see anywhere."

SIDECAR COCKTAIL

Ingredients

1. 2½ ounces cognac
2. ½ ounce triple sec
3. ¾ ounce lemon juice
4. Lemon peel twist for garnish
5. Lemon slice and sugar

Directions

1. Rub cocktail glass rim with lemon slice and sprinkle sugar on rim.

2. Put all other ingredients into shaker.
3. Add ample ice and shake vigorously.
4. Strain into glass and garnish with lemon twist.

LIPSTICK COCKTAIL

Ingredients

1. ⅔ ounce Bacardi light run
2. 1⅓ ounces grenadine
3. ⅔ ounce crème de bananes
4. 1⅓ ounces cream
5. Maraschino cherry for garnish

Directions

1. Fill shaker half full of ice.
2. Add first four ingredients.
3. Shake vigorously.
4. Strain into Old Fashioned glass with fresh ice.
5. Garnish with maraschino cherry and serve.

ORANGE SATCHMO

Ingredients

1. 2 ounces rye whiskey
2. 2 teaspoons triple sec
3. ¼ teaspoon absinthe
4. 1 dash Peychaud's bitters
5. Orange peel twist for garnish

Directions

1. Put rye, triple sec, and bitters into mixing glass.
2. Add ample ice and stir gently.
3. Put absinthe into chilled cocktail glass and coat the inside.
4. Strain mixing glass contents into cocktail glass.
5. Garnish with orange peel twist.

ARNOLD ROTHSTEIN COCKTAIL

Ingredients

1. 2 ounces gin
2. 2 teaspoons dry vermouth
3. 2 teaspoons Italian vermouth
4. 1 teaspoon maraschino liqueur
5. 2 dashes Angostura bitters
6. To garnish: on a stick, 1 brined olive, 1 maraschino cherry, 1 lemon peel twist

Directions

1. Put gin, both vermouths, and liqueur into mixing glass.
2. Add ample ice and stir gently.
3. Strain into cocktail glass, add bitters, and garnish.

CLOVER CLUB COCKTAIL

Ingredients

1. 1½ ounces dry gin
2. ½ ounce grenadine
3. ¾ ounce lemon juice
4. 1 teaspoon dry vermouth
5. 1 egg white
6. Maraschino cherry

Directions

1. Put first five ingredients into shaker.
2. Add ample ice.
3. Shake vigorously for thirty seconds.
4. Strain into chilled glass.
5. Garnish with cherry.

SLINGING SLANG

The slang that sprang up around the Roaring Twenties' cocktail culture owed its lineage to a literary forefather who did not imbibe. In his 1885 essay "Slang in America," the poet Walt Whitman reveled in yeasty new words that "fermented" in a country bubbling with energy from coast to coast. Slang had arisen, the essayist declared, "out of the work, needs, ties, joys, affections, and tastes of long generations of humanity." Sympathetic to temperance, Walt nonetheless shied away from the rigid rules that led to Volstead, insisting that a "lawless, germinal element" fueled all spirited speech, spoken and written. Writing in his own "barbaric yawp," Whitman had long scattered slang in poems that shocked devotées of Merriam-Webster's dictionaries. Meanwhile, the poet-lexicographer compiled an array of earthy terms he had picked up over a lifetime ("the Tennessee name for undiluted stimulant . . . Barefoot whiskey"). Against the dictums of schoolmasters and mistresses, Whitman stood his ground. Shakespeare, he found, had sided with slang.

Writers of the Roaring Twenties continued Whitman's practice of "wholesome fermentation." Like the poet, they steered clear of "bald literalism" and kept pace with the *vox populi*, ladling new coinages into the mix. In its 1920s heyday, *Time* magazine fostered a sometimes flippant tone dubbed "Timestyle" that tickled readers with such clever wordings as "politricks" and "tobacconalia."

Journalist and fiction writer Damon Runyon (b. 1880) found slang the perfect fit for the fractious temper of the 1920s. The portraitist of New York's demimonde of gamblers, bootleggers, sportsmen, and other assorted shady characters was best remembered for the short stories developed into the 1950 Broadway musical *Guys and Dolls* (and the 1955 film based on it, starring Marlon Brando and Jean Simmons). His hundreds of short stories in popular magazines (*Collier's*, *Saturday Evening Post*) were culled for bestselling books and thrust Runyon into the monetary stratosphere of US writers ($4,500 per story at his peak).

"Runyonesque" became the byword for the stew of slang and formal speech that became his trademark. A knife was a "shiv" and the head a "noggin." Young or old, Runyon's women were "dolls," and his characters' nicknames became allegories of identity, their stories always set in the present tense. Thus, the gambler Obadiah Masterson becomes "The Sky" because "he goes so high when it comes to betting. . . ." When The Sky's bet exceeds his funds, he must "take a run-out powder," meaning escape from "frozen-over"— i.e., wintry—Cincinnati.

If Damon Runyon sounds "dated" in the twenty-first century, Walt Whitman reminds us that slang's fermentation throws up "froth" that may "settle and permanently crystallize" or, more often, "mostly . . . pass away." The names of some 1920s cocktails, effervescent with topical slang at the time, beg for translation today.

FOUR FLUSHER (one who lives by sponging off others, or by pretense and fraud)

Ingredients

1. 1¼ ounces dry gin
2. ½ ounce vermouth
3. 1 teaspoon Dubonnet
4. ¼ teaspoon absinthe
5. 1 dash orange bitters
6. Maraschino cherry and orange peel twist

Directions

1. Put all ingredients except cherry and twist into shaker.
2. Add ample ice cubes and shake vigorously.
3. Strain into cocktail glass and garnish with cherry and twist.

THE CAT'S PAJAMAS (something or someone who is superlative)

Ingredients

1. 2 ounces gin
2. ¾ ounce triple sec or curaçao
3. 1 dash orange bitters
4. Orange peel twist for garnish

Directions

1. Put first two ingredients into mixing glass.
2. Add ample ice cubes and stir gently.
3. Strain into cocktail glass and add bitters.
4. Garnish with twist.

SAYS YOU! (exclamation of defiance)

Ingredients

1. 1 ounce scotch whisky
2. 2 teaspoons pineapple shrub
3. 2¼ ounces dry sparkling wine or champagne
4. Small pineapple wedge for garnish

Directions

1. Put first two ingredients into mixing glass.
2. Add ample ice cubes and stir gently.
3. Strain into champagne flute and top with wine or champagne.
4. Garnish with pineapple wedge.

ON A TOOT (on a spree, especially of drinking)

Ingredients

1. 1 ounce scotch whisky
2. ½ ounce Byrrh
3. 1 teaspoon maraschino liqueur
4. 1 dash orange bitters

5. Orange peel twist for garnish

Directions

1. Put first four ingredients into Old Fashioned glass.
2. Add ample ice cubes.
3. Stir gently and add garnish.

HORSEFEATHERS (nonsense, balderdash)

Ingredients

1. 1 ounce dark rum
2. 1 ounce cognac or brandy
3. ½ ounce Bénédictine
4. ½ ounce maraschino liqueur
5. Orange peel twist for garnish

Directions

1. Put first four ingredients into Old Fashioned glass.
2. Add ample ice cubes and stir gently.
3. Garnish with orange twist.

BEE'S KNEES (excellent, highly admired)

Ingredients

1. 2½ ounces gin
2. ¾ ounce honey syrup
3. ¾ ounce lemon juice
4. Honey
5. Lime slice for garnish

Directions

1. Put first three ingredients into mixing glass.
2. Add ample ice and shake vigorously.
3. Strain into cocktail glass that has been "drizzled" inside with honey.
4. Garnish with lime slice.

ON ALL SIXES (condition of confusion or disarray)

Ingredients

1. 2½ ounces gin
2. 2 teaspoons Swedish punsch
3. Mint sprig for garnish

Directions

1. Put gin and punsch into mixing glass.
2. Add ample ice cubes and stir gently.
3. Strain into cocktail glass.
4. Garnish with mint sprig.

GÉNÉRATION PERDUE

> All of you young people who served in the war. You are a
> lost generation.... You have no respect for anything. You
> drink yourselves to death.
>
> —Gertrude Stein, quoted by Ernest Hemingway

Indeed they drank, those American expatriates of the 1920s, occasionally taking a breather "on the wagon" when the bottle was shelved for a span of sobriety, but otherwise "tight," "smashed," or proudly "holding their liquor." Their roll call included men and women, but became largely synonymous with two Midwestern-born writers who rocketed to fame with fiction and lifestyles that captured the temper of the new times. Hemingway and Fitzgerald, Fitzgerald and Hemingway— acquaintances, "frenemies" of a sort, they defined the era.

As a young expatiate, Ernest Hemingway (b. 1899), a reporter for the Toronto *Star*, frequented the Paris studio of Gertrude Stein (b. 1874), the modernist writer and art collector who had lived in France since 1903 and famously declared, "America is my country, and Paris is my hometown." In the early 1920s, the California-raised Miss Stein held late afternoon salons at 27 Rue de Fleurus, where guests were served cakes and eau-de-vie in the apartment she shared with her companion, Alice B. Toklas, who chatted with Hemingway's wife, Hadley, while

Ernest studied the Cézannes, Manets, and Monets on Stein's walls and verbally jousted about the arts in talks with Stein. "There were almost never any pauses in a conversation with Miss Stein," Hemingway recalled, though he ultimately felt the two women "treated us as though we were very good, very well-mannered and promising children."

"Tall, muscular, broad-shouldered, and square-jawed," as his biographer Jeffrey Meyers describes him, the ambitious Hemingway's unwavering goal was to write serious fiction respected by the literary cognoscenti, especially its modernist pioneers James Joyce and Ezra Pound. His 1954 Nobel Prize in Literature was a quarter-century in the future when a story collection, *In Our Time* (1925), launched Hemingway's career. The stories were layered with battlefield scenes and recalled his experience as a WWI ambulance driver on the Italian front, including an injury that hospitalized Hemingway for months. His breakthrough novel, *The Sun Also Rises* (1926), reflected sportsman Hemingway's new-found fascination with bullfighting, to which he'd been introduced in Spain, and with his (and his characters') postwar self-medication with wine-or-spirits-at-all-times.

Scores of stories and esteemed novels followed as Hemingway's fame rose. His taut, linear sentences corresponded with the steel I-beam girders of the skyscraper and modernism's distaste for embellishment. As Hemingway recalled in his memoir, *A Moveable Feast*, "I found that I could cut that scrollwork or ornament out and start with the first true simple declarative sentence." In the final years of Prohibition, the celebrated writer lived in Key West, Florida, where he wrote the acclaimed *A Farewell to Arms* (1929), an antiwar novel that exemplified his writing style. Frederic Henry, the lead character, speaks for the author when he says, "You did not know what it was about. You never had time to learn. They threw you in and told you the rules, and the first time they caught you off base they killed you." Embarrassed by such hollowed-out terms as "sacred" and "sacrifice," the young man also rejects "abstract words such as glory, honor, courage or hallow," finding them nothing less than "obscene beside the concrete names of villages, the number of roads, the names of rivers, the numbers of regiments and the dates."

In Key West, Hemingway patronized a dive, the Blind Pig, a speakeasy where he could buy a few bottles of scotch from the proprietor, his friend Joe Russell, who opened a new bar, the Silver Slipper, on Greene and Duval Streets when the Eighteenth Amendment was repealed. The wet floors prompted Hemingway's suggestion that the place be renamed Sloppy Joe's; a favorite Key West oasis to this day, it is now the oldest licensed bar in the city.

* * *

Ernest Hemingway disliked F. Scott Fitzgerald on sight when the two met by chance at a Parisian café in 1924. Still a fledgling writer at the time, Hemingway was scrimping along as a newspaper reporter (supplemented by his wife's trust fund), and his hackles rose at the literary rival who had already won critical acclaim for bestselling novels and stories and now earned a good living as a professional writer. The two drank champagne that afternoon, and the talkative Fitzgerald struck Hemingway as boyish, "with a face between handsome and pretty . . . wavy hair, a high forehead, excited eyes and a delicate long-lipped Irish mouth." Fitzgerald's short legs kept him at medium height, Hemingway observed, and "his face was slightly puffy."

Fitzgerald nonetheless commended his literary discovery to his New York editor, Maxwell Perkins. ("This is to tell you about a young man named Ernest Hemingway who lives in Paris . . . and has a brilliant future. . . . He's the real thing.") Fitzgerald had already published an innovative, bestselling novel, *This Side of Paradise* (1920), portraying "a world in which all gods are dead, all wars fought and all faiths in man shaken," though the pages are subtly lightened by the several amours of the Princetonian leading character. Romantic love's pathology became a central theme of Fitzgerald's next novel, *The Beautiful and Damned* (1922). The saga of a marriage gradually collapsing in a haze of alcohol (a fictional forecast that friends feared might augur ill for the Fitzgeralds' own marriage), it included scenes of bacchanalian revels and such touches as the "three cases of Gordon gin" bought from a corrupt "revenue officer." Fitzgerald himself became the toast of New York City.

Two short story collections, *Flappers and Philosophers* (1920) and *Tales of the Jazz Age* (1922), likewise bestsellers, boosted Fitzgerald's celebrity, and the escapades of Scott and Zelda in Gotham fed gossip mills and set a new permissive standard for public conduct. Zelda had jumped into a fountain on Union Square, and Scott rode atop a taxi on Fifth Avenue. One admirer, Ernest Boyd, a literary man-about-town, marveled in 1924 that Scott Fitzgerald was "a character out of his own fiction" who "wrote the literature of which he is the incarnation." The Fitzgeralds, he continued, "appear as fresh and innocent and unspoiled as characters in the idyllic world of pure romance" and "with the impunity of their years can realize to the full all that the Jazz Age has to offer." Dorothy Parker added that the couple looked as though they had just stepped out of the sun.

The Fitzgeralds lived for months at New York's Plaza Hotel, then rented houses in Connecticut and Long Island, where weekend revels with friends turned into days-long bacchanalia that delayed Scott's work. Scott lamented that his $36,000 annual income (over half a million dollars today) could not meet expenses in the US, and his pleas for advances on royalties against future earnings grew embarrassing. Their money would go further in a Europe mired in a postwar depression, they decided, and in 1924, Scott and Zelda departed with their infant daughter, Frances Scott Fitzgerald, on a Cunard liner to France.

Ten years later, when Prohibition had ended, the Fitzgeralds co-authored an *Esquire* magazine piece, "Auction—Model 1934," which chronicled the couple's years as expatriates in Cannes, in Florence, in Venice, in the French Alps, in Rome. The cycle of fresh starts persisted through Zelda's fierce devotion to a belated ballet career and Scott's struggles with alcohol as he continued to work. In December 1925, he confessed to editor Perkins, "My work is the only thing that makes me happy—except to be a little tight—and for those two indulgences I pay price in mental and physical hangovers."

Readers of his next work, the classic novel *The Great Gatsby* (1925), sense the author's debt to the tradition of hard-edged fiction by Theodore Dreiser and Frank Norris, but find its pages rich with Fitzgerald's lush, unique Jazz Age styling. Here, for example, his oft-quoted lines describing a section of industrial Queens, New York: "This is a valley of ashes—a fantastic farm where ashes grow like wheat into ridges and hills and grotesque gardens, where ashes take the forms of houses and chimneys and rising smoke, and finally, with a transcendent effort, of men who move dimly and already crumbling through the powdery air." Cocktails abound in the novel, and the title character, Jay Gatsby, may rival Al Capone as America's most famous bootlegger.

Scott Fitzgerald's puckish side bubbled up in his 1926 letter of reply to a cocktail party invitation. The Jazz Age wordsmith declined with a clever conjugation of the verb "cocktail."

TO COCKTAIL
Present:
   I cocktail
   Thou cocktail
   It cocktails
   We cocktail
   You cocktail
   They cocktail

Imperfect: I was cocktailing
Perfect: I cocktailed (past definite)
Past perfect: I have cocktailed
Conditional: I might have cocktailed
Pluperfect: I had cocktailed
Subjunctive: I would have cocktailed
Voluntary Sub.: I should have cocktailed
Preterite: I did cocktail
Imperative: Cocktail!
Interrogative:
   Cocktailest thou?
   (Dos't Cocktail?)
   (or Wilt Cocktail?)
Subjunctive Conditional: I would have had to have
   cocktailed
Conditional Subjunctive: I might have had to have
   cocktailed
Participle: Cocktailing

Exponents of the Lost Generation, Francis Scott Key Fitzgerald of St. Paul, Minnesota, and Ernest Miller Hemingway of Oak Park, Illinois, left an enduring twentieth-century literary record, together with a Prohibition legacy worthy of a well-stocked bar. Scott often enjoyed Zelda's favorite Orange Blossom, and the drinks that punctuate his novels, essays, stories, and letters, include Prohibition's gin, claret, ale, Mint Julep, the Bronx, scotch, whiskey, wine, highballs, champagne, Chartreuse, Gin Rickeys, brandy, and French and Italian vermouths.

Hemingway's own cocktail sleuth, author Philip Greene, has masterfully chronicled young Ernest's libations from the kirsch he nipped after a day's writing (but prior to visiting Miss Stein), extending through the Key West years and onto the white-whiskered period of "Papa" Hemingway, when Prohibition had become, for most Americans, a distant memory.

ORANGE BLOSSOM

Ingredients

1. 2 ounces dry gin
2. Juice of one orange (2 ounces)

Directions

1. Put gin and orange juice into shaker.
2. Add ample ice.
3. Shake vigorously, strain, and serve in cocktail glass.

CHAMPAGNE COCKTAIL

Ingredients

1. 4–5 ounces chilled champagne
2. 1 sugar cube
3. Angostura bitters

Directions

1. Put sugar cube in champagne flute.
2. Saturate sugar with bitters.
3. Slowly fill flute with champagne.

GIN RICKEY

Ingredients

1. 2 ounces dry gin
2. ½ ounce fresh lime juice
3. 2–3 ounces seltzer water

Directions

1. In tall glass with ample ice cubes, add gin and lime juice.
2. Stir gently, add seltzer, and, once again, stir gently.
3. If desired, put in spent lime for garnish.

BLOODY MARY (à la Ernest Hemingway)

Ingredients

1. 1½ ounces vodka
2. 4 ounces tomato juice
3. ½ ounce fresh lemon (or lime) juice
4. 3 dashes Worcestershire sauce
5. Seasonings to taste (cayenne, celery salt)
6. Garnish to taste (celery stalk, pickled green bean or okra)

Directions

1. Put first five ingredients in shaker with ample ice.
2. Stir gently.
3. Transfer to highball glass and garnish as desired.

GLÜHWEIN

Ingredients

1. 1 quart dry red wine
2. Peel of 1 orange and 1 lemon
3. Spices (2–3 inches cinnamon stick, crushed whole nutmeg, 6 cloves)
4. 1 tablespoon sugar

Directions

1. Put all ingredients into large pot to simmer on stove.
2. Maintain simmer, tasting for preference.
3. When wine spiced to taste, remove from heat.
4. Strain spices and serve hot (serves eight).

HOT RUM PUNCH

Ingredients

1. 1½ bottles rum (each bottle 25.4 ounces)
2. 1 bottle cognac (25.4 ounces)
3. 3 quarts boiling water

4. 2 cups lemon juice

5. Brown sugar (to taste)

6. 6 cloves

Directions

1. Put all ingredients into large pot.

2. Simmer for thirty minutes, stirring occasionally.

3. Remove cloves.

4. Ladle into cups (serves forty).

BRANDY AND SODA

Ingredients

1. 2 ounces brandy

2. 4 ounces club soda or sparkling mineral water

Directions

1. Fill Collins glass with ice.

2. Add brandy and soda water.

3. Stir gently.

TO THE LOST

Ingredients

1. 2 ounces scotch whisky

2. 2 teaspoons ginger syrup

3. 1 dash Peychaud's bitters

4. 1 dash Angostura bitters

5. Orange slice for garnish

Directions

1. Put whisky and syrup into mixing glass.

2. Add ample ice and stir gently.

3. Strain into cocktail glass and add bitters.

4. Garnish with orange slice.

WHEELS

If dudes and flappers endured old timers' accounts of the "horseless carriage" and its formidable hand-crank ignition that broke wrists, by the 1920s, every customer who eyed new car models in a dealer's showroom took for granted an electric starter, electric windshield wipers, a laminated safety-glass windshield, and headlamps for night driving. Salesmen touted the newest models with heaters, balloon tires, and shock absorbers to banish bone-rattling drives. Bowing to personal taste, they bragged that the dominant funereal black had yielded to the automakers' vibrant colors on display before them—deep greens, lustrous browns, carnelian reds. (In 1926, Henry Ford rescinded his dictum: "A customer can have a car painted any color he wants as long as it's black.")

The 1920s younger motorists preferred the short, snappy "auto" or "car" over the elders' "machine," "motor car," or "automobile" (these last two continuing to be cherished by dealers in high-end models). The Ford "Model T" (aka "Tin Lizzie") and Model "A" still dotted the roadways, but the low-slung modern cars featured sleek silhouettes and more powerful engines. A garden-variety auto's top speed averaged about forty-five mph, while a high-end model, such as a Lincoln, Cadillac, or Packard, could reach sixty mph with ease. (Not surprisingly, Prohibition's gangland chiefs opted for deluxe, custom-armored versions. New York's Frankie Yale chose a Lincoln, while Chicago's Al Capone selected a "seven-ton rolling fortress" of a Cadillac.)

Advertisers and creative writers vied to capture the sensuous profile of the latest in automotive design, from the adman's Lincoln that "merits confidence and pride" to novelist Sinclair Lewis's "streamlined DeSoto." F. Scott Fitzgerald most probably had in mind a Daimler-Benz touring car in his epoch description of Gatsby's vehicle in *The Great Gatsby*: "It was a rich cream color, bright with nickel, swollen here and there in its monstrous length with triumphant hatboxes and supper-boxes and tool-boxes, and terraced with a labyrinth of windshields that mirrored a dozen suns." Fitzgerald added a "green leather conservatory" of sumptuous seats to the much-too-much car, inviting the reader to hop in for a spin. (*The Great Gatsby*'s dark storyline also features an oily used-car garage, auto mishaps by drivers under the influence, and a heart-wrenching fatality involving the cream-colored car.)

Rocky, rutted roadways often thwarted streamlined driving in the 1920s, and gravel still topped most roads. Upton Sinclair's *Oil!* (1927) opens with a paean to pavement, a promise to the future. Cruising a California highway with his father at the wheel, a young man in the passenger seat glories in the open road, "smooth and flawless . . . a ribbon of grey concrete." One could climb hills without fear, he muses, "for you knew the magic ribbon would be there, clear of obstructions, unmarred by bump or scar, waiting the passage of inflated rubber wheels." The "magic ribbon" gave way to the "Main Street of America" on November 11, 1926, in a celebration honoring the completion of US Route 66, the two-lane highway that ran from Chicago to Los Angeles, stretching through Missouri, Kansas, Oklahoma, Texas, New Mexico, and Arizona, continuing to Santa Monica, California, in the LA area, a distance of 2,448 miles. Auto tourists vacationing along Route 66 found gas stations, eateries, and lodgings created just for them, the motor hotels soon dubbed "motels." (Nobel Prize–winning novelist John Steinbeck memorialized this "Mother Road" in his 1939 epic, *The Grapes of Wrath*, and the interstate highway Route 40 roughly parallels the classic Route 66.)

When asked "what's changing the country?" a 1920s Midwesterner spelled this answer: "A-U-T-O." The cocktail might precede Prohibition, but the "dry decade" lubricated both car and driver.

THE AUTOMOBILE COCKTAIL

Ingredients

1. 1 ounce gin
2. 1 ounce scotch whisky
3. ¾ ounce Italian (sweet) vermouth
4. 1 dash orange bitters

Directions

1. In mixing glass, add all ingredients.
2. Add cubed ice.
3. Stir thoroughly.
4. Strain and serve in cocktail glass.

RUM-RUNNERS, RUM ROW, AND THE REAL McCOY

In July 1921, the New York news-papers reported a flotilla of ships spotted off the Northeast coast, their sails furled and sleek hulls at anchor. The "strange" vessels appeared to be selling liquor, a trade forbidden since the Volstead Act had taken effect over eighteen months earlier. To many, this news came as a welcome relief. Like castaways on a desert island, imbibers hailed the overseas rescuers, arriving with liquors bottled in bond, distilled in Scotland or Ireland and properly aged for years in charred oak barrels. Flagged from foreign countries, the ships also brought Jamaican rum, rare brandies, and effervescent wines from French champagne country. Such precious cargo, the purveyors asserted, meant "the real thing . . . off the boat."

The slogan would soon ring hollow. By the late 1920s, rum-running would be controlled by syndicates comparable to the rich, resourceful, and ruthless modern-day drug cartels. The onboard liquors would already have been "cut," diluted, and adulterated to multiply the bootleggers' profits. Countless cases of aged liquors, once ashore, were sent first to "cutting plants" before selling at the highest prices to credulous consumers. In the beginning, however, the somewhat romantic, if risky, enterprise involved adventurous mariners, local fishermen, nearby farmers, car and truck drivers, and one celebrated skipper, William (Bill) McCoy, for whom the phrase "the real McCoy" rang true.

Rum Rows sprang up along all US coastlines with the onset of Prohibition, ranging north and south between Vancouver and the Mexican border, and extending all along the Gulf of Mexico. The most traveled Whiskey Road, however, was a sea lane arching between New York's coastal waters and the Bahamas, Cuba, and Jamaica, always outside twelve-mile US territorial waters and thus beyond the reach of the US Coast Guard. The Caribbean islands boasted the busiest Rum Row ports, and the British-ruled Bahamas, geographic "kissing cousins" to Florida and points north, became a favorite hub for anyone with a boat and a motor. Patrolled with British decorum by islander constables in "white sun helmets, white cotton tunics, cotton gloves, and dark blue trousers," Nassau's Bay Street became "Booze Avenue." To avoid legally ensnaring bank records, rum-running deals were cash only, sealed by coded telegrams and "gentlemen's" handshakes.

With its "profusion of inlets, rivers, coves, and mangrove swamps," Florida's topography invited smuggling, plus decent roads for distribution. Bimini, at forty-five miles from Miami, or Grand Bahama Island, a mere fifty-five miles from Palm Beach, or Cuba, just ninety miles from the Florida shores—these boomed as a "liquid gold triangle." While syndicates swiftly moved in to rule the liquor empire, small-time rum-runners overloaded flimsy motorboats, crossed choppy open waters all night long, and putt-putted into shoreline mangrove thickets before dawn, hoping to evade armed hijackers and praying that their cargo would be intact for retrieval in the morning.

Often the precious stacked-up cases would be stolen by "pelicans," thieves who hid in the mangroves, risked nothing, but simply waited, watched, and pounced for booty. Among the "pelicans" lurked corrupt revenue agents who knew that each four-dollar case of rum, for instance, could fetch a peak price of one hundred dollars.

Rum ships also loaded up in maritime Canada, Newfoundland, and the French St. Pierre Island—all governed by nations in which legal alcoholic beverages were taxed to enhance revenue. As long as taxes were paid, the destinations of the products were of no official concern, and cargos of liquors and wines could be stowed below decks, safe and snug, to earn a vessel the simple nickname, rum ship.

In *Confessions of a Rum Runner* (1928), the British adventurer James Barbican—a pseudonym for the Oxford-educated Eric Sherbrooke Walker (b. 1887)—provided an inside look at the volatile trade, which he first explored over drinks in London with an experienced captain after applying "a little judicious flattery, combined with the right number of drinks." From his loquacious companion, "Barbi" learned that an onshore order was placed at an agreed-upon price, then a chartered rum ship was loaded and captained by a skilled seaman—such as himself—and a crew eager for well-paying jobs. Also aboard, an important employee, a "supercargo," who represented the owner of the cargo of liquors and wines. He would oversee the cases stowed in the ship's hold and count each case during the offloading when the ship reached its destination. He would receive and count the cash payment and disburse other monies from the moment the ship left the dock until it reached its home port. If a supercargo were unavailable, his duties fell to the captain. Either way, the crew would flourish and the captain enjoy a most bountiful reward.

"Barbi," something of a soldier of fortune (having been a WWI flyer), was intrigued by the details. He learned that the rum ship sailed into waters miles off the agreed-on coastal site, say, twenty-five

miles off New Jersey, and waited to be sighted (sometimes spotted by aircraft reconnaissance). A fleet of fast contact boats—sometimes local fishermen—would then speed from the shore to the ship, where the contraband booze would be offloaded into the boats and paid for with a thick roll of cash tossed up to the supercargo or captain. (If questioned, the "fishermen" vowed they were going out for herring or cod.) The supercargo counted the money, signaled all was "jake," and sent the liquor-loaded small boats speeding ashore in hopes that they would reach the safe shallows where any Coast Guard cutters in pursuit would run aground.

Once the cargo in the boats reached the shore, hired hands would transfer each case to the barn of a farmer who earned storage "hay" at a dollar or two per case. Soon, the farmer's barn-turned-warehouse would be visited by cars and trucks to speed the whiskies and wines to their next destination. All this would take place in darkness. Neither the ship, the speedboats, nor the motor vehicles operated with lights or radio contact. Meantime, the empty rum ship would be homeward bound, and the supercargo or captain would pay the crew and be ready to settle with the distiller or whoever had owned the liquors and wines. The next deal would soon be arranged, the next load, the next voyage.

The captain's account made rum-running "seem simple enough," a straightforward and highly profitable venture. Barbican was warned, however, about onshore gangs of "hijackers" who struck at dusk, just when the fleet of fast contact boats was expected at the ship. Hijackers struck hard and fast. If binoculars showed the onrushing boats bristling with guns, the ship's captain must distribute firearms to his crew and order the deck-mounted machine gun to be readied for firing. "There is no redress against them," Barbican was warned, "for it is a case of 'dog-eat-dog.' They are outside the law, and so are you."

For the next two years, 1924–26, Captain Barbican of the yacht *Istar* learned firsthand the perils of rum-running in Atlantic seas, including engine troubles and winter storms that iced the decks and hemp lines. Food and water sometimes ran low, and the restless crew's near-mutinous anger boiled. If the liquor were not securely stowed below, a few bottles broke in heavy seas, and the crew eagerly consumed the contents of the case as "salvage," sometimes brawling afterward. One major hazard in the New York–New Jersey waters: collisions with other vessels. Sailors called the area "Broadway and Forty-Second Street" due to the hundreds of ships that routinely plied these waters, from passenger liners to tankers and colliers.

The vulnerable rum-runners "carried no anchor lights, rang no bells," and sounded no foghorns in case of nearby Coast Guard patrols. Collision meant the "crunch of impact," the "quick grind of disintegration," and the vague "random cry" that became a haunting, lifelong memory for survivors.

One more peril lurked: the cash payment for the shipment. Alongside the rum ship, the speedy contact boats' motors roared as the cargo was transferred from the ship's hold to the deck and down to the boats bobbing below. "The names of brands and amounts were shouted," and "a roll of big-denomination bills held together by an elastic band was pitched aboard." Quickly counting in the darkness, the captain or supercargo "could do no more than squint" at the bills, hoping they were not counterfeit and trusting that the roll was not worthless paper covered over with a single thousand-dollar bill.

Captain Barbican took the risks and learned the lessons, and so did Captain William (Bill) McCoy (b. 1877), who had loved the sea from boyhood, when he first set eyes on the graceful training ship *Saratoga*, at anchor in the Delaware River off the Philadelphia waterfront. Two years as a cadet on the ship earned McCoy a third-mate's license, but he opted for jobs on yachts and coastal steamers instead of the slower merchant marine vessels. In 1900, he relocated to Jacksonville, Florida, where he partnered with his brother, who had opened a boatyard. The McCoy brothers' motorboats earned high marks for workmanship, and the boatyard thrived.

His neighbors seemed to be just as prosperous. Bill McCoy was stunned in early 1920 when a formerly down-at-the-heels fisherman turned up wearing "Palm Beach specialty-shop clothes, smoking a dollar cigar and driving a long and high-priced roadster." Few sailors in the area could handle a schooner under sail, and Atlantic City, New Jersey, needed its shipment of rye whiskey that was due from Nassau in the Bahamas. The American liquor market was expanding all the time. Never mind Prohibition. Would Bill care to earn a hundred dollars a day?

Bill McCoy turned the offer down, but a life at sea beckoned, and a zest for serious money spurred him to sell his share of the boatyard and purchase a ninety-foot schooner, *Henry L. Marshall*, at a New England shipyard. At $16,000, plus another $4,000 for refitting, the vessel was readied for all weathers. Below decks, the schooner would hold its liquor. The boat proved true when McCoy took the helm and pointed the bow toward Nassau, where liquor wholesalers waited to charter such a craft.

The *Marshall* began its new career with a load of fifteen hundred cases of Old Grand-Dad bourbon that McCoy ran successfully from the Caribbean to New York. Back in Nassau, he bypassed the gangsters brandishing .38s and blackjacks and shook hands with an Italian outfit that needed to send Hill and Hill brand Kentucky bourbon to Long Island. Another voyage, another success—and Bill McCoy made enough money to buy a gorgeous schooner he had eyed in New England, the *Arethusa*. With new rigging and sails, she could carry five thousand cases per trip. (For British registry, he renamed her *Tomoka*.) Bill McCoy is credited with an ingenious idea for repackaging liquor, which distillers insisted on crating in wooden boxes that took up far too much space. He hired Bahamian women to repack the bottles in six-bottle pyramids—three at the bottom, then two, then one—all six tightly packed in straw, bundled in burlap, and tied with heavy twine into a familiar shape nicknamed a "ham."

As both captain and owner of the *Tomoka*, the *Marshall*, and, quite soon, five other vessels, and with crews to hire and support, McCoy had rapidly expanded his business, which led to his undoing. The *Marshall*, under the command of a hired captain, was seized off Atlantic City with fifteen hundred cases of whiskey (three thousand "hams") and registered to William McCoy, who was accurately reputed to own other rum-running vessels. With newer, faster boats, such as the cutter *Seneca*, in November 1923, the Guard issued orders for McCoy's capture, even in international waters. At the helm of the *Tomoka*, McCoy hoisted full sail, but soon surrendered. Pleading guilty to avoid a long, costly trial, Bill McCoy served nine months in prison, abandoned rum-running, and spent the rest of his life in Florida.

Imbibers had reason to especially mourn McCoy's departure from the business. In an era of loose standards and fast bucks, liquor from a McCoy's stock was guaranteed to be the real thing, never "cut," never watered down. Bill earned a reputation for shipping clean liquor. Every bottle off his vessel was, reliably, "the real McCoy." Today, signature cocktails still recall the rum-runners' offshore whereabouts, the "fishermen's" alibis, and the Caribbean ports.

TWELVE MILES OUT

Ingredients

1. 1 ounce white rum
2. 1 ounce calvados
3. ½ ounce Cocchi Americano
4. 1 teaspoon clove syrup
5. Lemon peel twist

Directions

1. Put first four ingredients in mixing glass.
2. Add ample ice and stir gently.
3. Strain into Old Fashioned glass with ice.
4. Garnish with lemon twist.

FISHING TRIP

Ingredients

1. 1 ounce bourbon

2. 1 ounce Swedish punsch

3. 1 ounce orange juice

4. 3½ ounces soda water

5. Orange slice for garnish

Directions

1. Put first three ingredients into mixing glass.

2. Add ample ice cubes and stir gently.

3. Strain into tall glass with fresh ice cubes.

4. Top with soda water and garnish with orange slice.

EVERYTHING'S "JAKE"

Ingredients

1. 1 ounce tequila

2. 2 ounces Swedish punsch

3. Small pineapple wedge for garnish

Directions

1. Put tequila and punsch into mixing glass.

2. Add ample ice and stir gently.

3. Strain into cocktail glass and garnish with pineapple.

BACARDI COCKTAIL

Ingredients

1. 2 ounces Bacardi rum

2. 1 ounce gin

3. 1 teaspoon grenadine

4. Juice of ½ lime

Directions

1. Put ingredients into mixing glass.

2. Add ample ice and stir gently.

3. Strain into cocktail glass.

KINGSTON COOLER

Ingredients

1. 1 ounce dark rum
2. ½ ounce dry vermouth
3. ½ ounce cherry brandy
4. 2 teaspoons lime juice
5. 5 ounces soda water
6. Lime slice for garnish

Directions

1. Put first four ingredients in a shaker.
2. Add ample ice and shake vigorously.
3. Strain into tall glass.
4. Add large lump of ice and top with soda water.
5. Garnish with lime slice.

BOOTLEGGING LADIES

In August 1920, feminists cheered the passage of the Nineteenth Amendment to the US Constitution, which granted nationwide female suffrage, but three enterprising American women cheered the amendment that had, seven months earlier, banned alcoholic beverages. The Volstead law promised sobriety and prompted celebration in "dry" quarters, but these three women rejoiced for reasons of their own. The Volstead Act freed them to "vote" in favor of bootlegging. Perhaps they would venture to the polls to cast presidential ballots for Warren G. Harding in 1924 or Calvin Coolidge in 1928, but probably not. Every waking hour found them busy at their new tradecraft: booze.

Throughout the 1920s, the "tall, slender, black-haired" Ohio-born Gertrude ("Cleo") Lythgoe supplied liquor on order from the Bahamas, while the blue-eyed Marie Waite (nicknamed "Spanish Marie") helped her rum-runner husband and, after his death, ran a strict rum-running empire between Havana and south Florida. In the Northeast, meanwhile, the dark-haired, "rosy-complexioned" Maisie Manders fulfilled orders from her Packard motor car, custom-fitted with heavy-duty springs to support the weighty cargo. All three flourished, although Marie's and Gertrude's brushes with the law became a matter of record. Neither served time in jail. Prohibition served them well, and they returned the favor.

Nicknamed "Cleo" for her imagined resemblance to the Egyptian queen, Gertrude Lythgoe (b. 1888) had been rescued from an Ohio orphanage by an aunt who supported her niece's schooling, including the clerical studies that often enabled a single woman's self-support in the early twentieth century. Her jobs as a skilled stenographer in California and New York led to Gertrude's employment by a London liquor exporter who seized the opportunity to supply Prohibition-era America with its desired whiskies, including the McTavish and Haig brands of scotch. Gertrude, as the London office knew, was smart and savvy, and the exporter tapped her to operate the business from Nassau, some three hundred miles from Florida in the British-ruled Bahama Islands, where alcoholic beverages were legal. A reporter described her as a "truly a wonderful personality, a woman of cultivated tastes who can talk about books and who travels with the best music in her trunks, and shows artistic taste in dress."

But Cleo was no soft touch. She once tracked down a man who made "derogatory" remarks about the products she shipped and about her too. Finding him lathered for a shave in a barber's chair, she "fetched" him along to her office "for a talk." "Everyone knows that my liquor is the very best," she said. "I just warned him. I told him I'd put a bullet through him as sure as he sat there." He fled. (One or two mobsters recalled this "Bahama Queen" jamming a pistol "into their ribs by way of making things clear.") On one occasion, Cleo sailed for several weeks off the New York coast aboard bootlegger Bill McCoy's rum-running yacht, *Tomoka*, which was loaded with her company's contraband liquor. McCoy fell hard for the "Bahama Queen," but she slipped away to live in Miami, New York, and Detroit until her death in Los Angeles in 1974 at eighty-six years of age.

By reputation, "Cleo" Lythgoe surely knew of the Havana-based "Spanish Marie" Waite, who entered the business in 1926 when a man's body—that of her rum-runner husband, Charlie Waite—"washed ashore" on Florida's Key Biscayne. The Coast Guard, responsible for her husband's death, became her enemy, and outwitting or outrunning its patrols became her primary aim. The tall widow with "a hot Latin temperament" set up shop in Havana to "ruthlessly rule a rum running empire" from the island nation of Cuba, where Bacardi distilled fine spirits and alcoholic beverages were legal. (Bacardi's taunting invitation to US mainlanders during Prohibition: "Come to Cuba, and bathe in Bacardi rum.")

A smart businesswoman dubbed the "female admiral," Spanish Marie commanded a flotilla of fifteen speedboats, running rum and other spirits from Cuba to Key West and Palm Beach at a fast twenty to thirty knots. She dispatched her cargo in convoys of four boats, three loaded with liquor, the fourth "armed to the teeth" to protect the others and, as necessary, to take on a Coast Guard cutter and allow the other three to escape for on-time deliveries in south Florida. Radio transmissions in coded Spanish let Marie's boats evade patrols, but in May 1928, she and her crew were caught unloading contraband wines and spirits near Miami. Arrested and scheduled for a court date, Marie Waite posted bail, disappeared, and was never brought to justice. The inventory seized during her arrest—"whisky, rum, gin, wine, champagne, and beer"—provides a keyhole view into the size of her empire. The number of bottles seized that day: 5,526.

While nowhere as dramatic as speedboats, rum-running yachts, or airplanes circling overhead with bottles in the fuselage, the risky,

touch-and-go job of smuggling bottles secretly stashed in farmers' barns for scheduled pickups by trucks and autos required a motorized fleet and drivers with nerves of steel. With a cool head and steady hands at the wheel. Maisie Mander, no mere driver for hire, ran her one-woman business supplying customers from mansions to speakeasies by transporting hooch from storage barns to their final destinations in her Packard coupé.

This Prohibition road warrior could hide thirty dozen bottles under her seats and floorboards. Arriving at a barn or other "stash" house in darkness, the "plump and determined" Maisie, "clad in a fur coat and a smart little hat," climbed inside the back of her car, took two or three bottles handed to her at a time, including champagne, and "packed them neatly, neck to neck," protecting them with layers of straw and filling the car in less than an hour. Carefully removing all traces of telltale straw from the running boards, she jumped into the driver's seat, cranked up the windows, locked both doors from inside, and drove into the pitch-black night, often for hours.

"It would take a can-opener to get me out of here once I am in," she declared. "When I am locked in my coupé, they would have to smash up the car to get at me, and it would take a real tough guy to do that to a good-looking young lady like me. . . . Besides, I might not wait for them to try." Recalled a British male admirer, also in the business, "Day and night, she would tear over those roads all alone. I have seen her pull in at two o'clock in the morning when everyone was asleep and just curl up in the seat of her great car and sleep peacefully. . . . A tough little Yank she is, and I always liked her for her hardihood."

CHAMPAGNE JULEP

Ingredients
1. 2–3 ounces champagne (brut)
2. Sprig of fresh mint
3. 1 lump sugar
4. 1 lump ice

Directions
1. Put sugar, ice, and mint into large wine glass.
2. At the same time, add champagne very slowly.
3. Garnish with seasonal fresh fruit.

HAVANA SMILE

Ingredients

1. 1½ ounces Bacardi rum
2. 1½ ounces Italian vermouth
3. ½ teaspoon sugar
4. ½ teaspoon lime juice

Directions

1. Put ingredients into mixing glass.
2. Stir gently (until sugar dissolves).
3. Add ice and stir again.
4. Strain into cocktail glass.

CAMERON'S KICK COCKTAIL

Ingredients

1. 1 ounce scotch whisky
2. 1 ounce Irish whiskey
3. 1 ounce lemon juice
4. 2 ounces orgeat (almond) syrup

Directions

1. Put ingredients into mixing glass.
2. Add ample ice and stir moderately.
3. Strain and serve in cocktail glass.

DRINK, DRANK, DRUNK

In 1737, Benjamin Franklin published his *Drinker's Dictionary*, a slender volume hedged with caution against "DRUNKENNESS, a very unfortunate Vice," but brimming with synonyms for a state of inebriation (among others, "Addled," "Crack'd," and "Got a Brass Eye"). Franklin sealed the tippler's fate in a *Poor Richard's Almanack* aphorism: "Nothing more like a Fool than a drunken Man." Foolish or sage, two centuries later, Prohibition vastly overtopped the teetotaling Franklin's lexical predecessor. A mere sampling from Edmund Wilson's "Lexicon of Prohibition" provides nicknames for every state of inebriation "beginning with the mildest stages and progressing to the more disastrous."

Bleary-eyed	Boiled
Blind	Boiled as an owl
Bloated	Buried
Blotto	Canned

Cock-eyed
Corked
Corned
Crocked
Edged
Embalmed
Featured
Four sheets in the wind
Fried
Fried to the hat
Full
Full as a tick
Glassy-eyed
Half-cocked
Half-screwed
Half-shot
Half seas over
Happy
High
Hoary-eyed
Hooted
Horseback
Jagged
Jazzed
Jingled
Lathered
Leaping
Liquored
Lit
Loaded
Loaded for bear

Loaded to the muzzle
Lubricated
Oiled
Organized
Ossified
Out like a light
Over the bay
Owled
Paralyzed
Passed out cold
Pickled
Pie-eyed
Piffed
Piped
Plastered
Polluted
Potted
Primed
Saturated
Scrooched
Shicker (Yiddish)
Shreeching
Slopped
Slopped to the ears
Sloppy
Soused
Spifflicated
Sprung
Squiffy
Stewed
Stewed to the fills [gills?]

Stiff
Stinko
Tanked
Tight
Under the Table
Wall-eyed
Wapsed down [?]
Wet
Woozy
Zozzled

Lit up like the sky
Lit up like the
    Commonwealth
Lit up like a Christmas tree
Lit up like a store window
Lit up like a church
To have a bun on
To have a slant on

To have a skate on
To have a snootful
To have a skinful
To draw a blank
To pull a shut-eye
To pull a Daniel Boone
To have a rubber drink
To have a hangover
To have a head
To have the jumps
To have the shakes
To have the zings
To have the heeby-jeebies
To have the
    screaming-meemies
To have the whoops and
    jingles
To burn with a low blue
    flame

WINGING IT

Dreams of flight have tantalized human beings since *Homo sapiens* first gazed skyward to marvel at creatures powered by feathery wings. In Greek myth, the father-son duo of Daedalus and Icarus took flight to escape the island of Crete until the son's wax wings melted in the sun, but the cautionary tale of hubris and a deadly plunge into the sea did not discourage Renaissance engineering genius Leonardo da Vinci from drafting his own plans for human flight. His fifteenth-century *Codex on the Flight of Birds* featured detailed designs for a flying machine based on the movements of birds' wings, and for centuries, those flapping wings seemed the key to flight—until the internal combustion engine opened new possibilities. European inventors went to work, and two American brothers from Ohio dreamed, studied, and put their lessons into practice on the Atlantic coast.

When bicycle mechanics Orville (b. 1871) and Wilbur (b. 1867) Wright lofted their engine-powered, muslin-covered, spruce-framed contraption, the *Wright Flyer*, into freezing headwinds over Kitty

Hawk, North Carolina, in December 1903—their twelve-horsepower aeroplane flew just 120 feet off the ground—Charles Lindbergh (b. 1902) was a ten-month-old infant, and Amelia Earhart (b. 1897) a half-year shy of her sixth birthday. Earhart and Lindbergh would both appear on *Time* magazine covers as persons of the year—Lindbergh in 1927, Earhart labeled "Intrepid Aviator" in 1932—both having taken their place among scores of pilots who flew for adventure, for the US mail, for crop dusting, for the military, and for business that shipped cargo and carried adventurous passengers into the sky on routes that shrunk terrestrial travel time by head-spinning margins.

Pilots of the early 1920s, among them Earhart and Lindbergh, included amateur hobbyists organized in flying clubs, such as the Aero Club of Southern California, together with veterans discharged from the US Army Air Service. In civilian life, the former "aces" adapted tactical flight skills learned in reconnaissance, bombardment, and aerial combat known as "dogfighting" (e.g., lobbing hand grenades at an enemy's plane, before belt-link ammunition made aerial gunnery a lethal reality). (Charles Schultz's *Peanuts* comic strip features imagined dogfights pitting Snoopy, the endearing beagle, against the German Red Baron.) After the November 1918 armistice, war-surplus planes moved into private hands and also found service as trainers at flight schools such as the Nebraska Aircraft Corporation, where Charles Lindbergh took lessons in the hope that flying could replace the college studies he found so tedious.

For a time, Lindbergh joined the barnstorming pilots who performed aerial stunts for audiences who gathered in open fields or cow pastures to gawk at takeoffs and then, all eyes skyward, to gaze in wonder at the circus in the clouds: acrobatic loop the loops, barrel rolls, dives, wing walks, and other daredevil stunts. The early 1920s barnstormers toured the country like vagabonds, scraping by on income from onlookers who paid to be taken aloft (five dollars per ride).

Outfitted in leather flight helmets, jodhpurs, high-top boots, and flowing white silk neck scarves, the pilots cut a romantic figure, and their stunts grew ever bolder to please easily jaded audiences.

A few women joined their ranks, such as twenty-four-year-old African American pilot Bessie Coleman (b. 1896). Rebuffed by US flight instructors in racist Jim Crow America, she quit her manicurist job in Chicago, traveled to France, became a licensed pilot, and barnstormed in the States—but only for desegregated audiences. From his biplane, "Daredevil Lindbergh" perfected parachuting to earth, and Southern California's Long Beach Air Rodeo featured two planes flying in close parallel to each other, while a wing walker stepped from one to the other, plane-to-plane in midair.

The perils did not faze those determined to take wing, including passengers lured by the promise of shortened travel time. In the early 1920s, two airlines began operating flights between London and Paris, and in August 1922, a young American reporter on assignment for the Toronto *Star* found that a railway journey of ten hours could be cut to one hour and a half if he traveled from Paris to Strasbourg by air. Accompanied by his wife, Hadley, the twenty-three-year-old Ernest Hemingway described for *Star* readers "bicyclists on the road looking like pennies rolling along a narrow white strip. . . . Gray red-roofed towns . . . old trenches zigzagging through a field pocked with shell holes." In the cabin, Hadley sat hunched in her fur coat with cotton plugs in her ears, but Ernest stayed glued to the sights below. When the plane dipped to avoid a storm, "close to the ground . . . we followed a canal that we could see below us through the rain. . . . The plane headed high out of the storm into the bright sunlight and we saw the flat, tree-lined muddy ribbon of the Rhine." Hadley soon returned to Paris, but Ernest stayed on in Germany, where his income made a five-course meal an occasional affordable expense. (The young journalist did not detail the dishes or drinks he savored, but a good bet would be the Asbach brandy cocktail.)

Hemingway's journalist pals had refused to fly, with good reason. The previous month, four passengers and the pilot had died on the same route he and Hadley had flown, and another plane on that path had crash-landed when the engine stalled, injuring everyone aboard. US newspapers reported an alarming number of rickety planes that crashed on takeoff or landing and sometimes fell from the sky when their engines suddenly failed. Ormer Locklear, the "greatest of all daredevil fliers" (and the first to perform aerial stunts in films), perished near Hollywood in 1920 when his plane spiraled in a fatal tailspin. Laura Bromwell, a "foremost American aviatrix," crashed to her death off Long Island, New York, in the summer of 1921. Amelia Earhart's biographer, Susan Butler, notes that by 1920, "the year Amelia fell in love with flying," fifteen US aerial mail pilots had died.

By 1926, Charles Lindbergh was becoming bored flying the US mail at three dollars per pound on a St. Louis–Chicago route. A small company had won the government contract that put the young pilot into the cockpit of a war-surplus De Havilland plane for five weekly round trips from St. Louis to Chicago. (Passage of the 1925 Air Mail Act transferred air mail from the Post Office to private contractors.) The former barnstormer had more recently sharpened his flight skills as a commissioned officer in the Army Air Service Reserve Corps, an enlistment that put Lindbergh into planes that would "roar up into the sky." The De Havilland mail plane did not roar, and the weekly runs gave Lindbergh ample time to envision "a solo flight across the North Atlantic." In 1919, a New York hotelier, Raymond Orteig, had offered a prize of $25,000 for a nonstop flight across the Atlantic Ocean. Experienced aviators had perished in the pursuit, but the prize had not been claimed.

Charles Lindbergh's stupendous solo flight in the *Spirit of St. Louis* in May 1927 won the Orteig prize money—and the worldwide adoration of millions. The feat earned the twenty-five-year-old pilot the nickname "Lucky Lindy," but the effort required meticulous planning.

Named for Lindbergh's financial backers in St. Louis, the *Spirit* demanded experts in engine mechanics, aerodynamics, and fabrication. The sleek plane took shape at Ryan Airlines in San Diego, and the team welcomed Lindbergh's hands-on input. A month before the May 21–22 flight to Paris, he flew the *Spirit* from the West Coast to New York, stopping along the way as he grew accustomed to the aircraft powered by a 223-horsepower, nine-cylinder engine in a plane weighing 5,250 pounds when fueled by 450 gallons of gasoline (courtesy of Standard Oil).

Draconian efficiencies ruled every decision about the plane, the pilot, and his equipment. The flight of thirty-three and one-half hours over a distance of 3,610 miles required a delicate balance of fuel versus weight. Safety could take second place to fuel efficiency. Should Lindbergh ditch in the ocean, there would be no heavy inflatable life raft. Nor would a back-up pilot be aboard. Lindbergh said, "I'd rather have the extra gasoline than an extra man."

The *Spirit*'s cockpit put him in a lightweight cushioned wicker seat in an upright position, while a celluloid skylight above his head allowed the stars to provide navigational help, and a periscope let him see the earth, the water, and the clouds. The "Lone Eagle" donned his leather flight helmet and a wool-insulated flight suit. Underneath, he wore a light jacket, a white shirt, and a red-and-white striped necktie. An army officer's riding breeches and US Cavalry officer's boots completed the outfit.

Among the challenges of winds, navigation, icing, and countless unforeseen obstacles, one factor loomed as large as all others: the need to stay awake with a clear mind at all times. Frequent entries in a log would help with mental discipline, so the logbook was worthwhile weight. Some would dub Lindbergh "Lucky Lindy," but others feared he was to become the "Flying Fool."

"Pandemonium" erupted on May 22, 1927, when the *Spirit of St. Louis* touched down at the Le Bourget Aerodrome in Paris at 10:22

p.m. Some one hundred thousand French citizens rushed across the field to greet his plane and clawed for souvenirs. The *Spirit* was secured, and Charles Lindbergh instantly became the most famous man on earth, cheered by a half-million French citizens when honored by a parade along the Champs-Élysées, awarded a gold key to the city, and personally promised the $25,000 prize on a handshake by Raymond Orteig, who happened to be in France. Lindbergh then flew the *Spirit* to Belgium and on to London, mobbed by admirers at each stop.

For the return journey, the *Spirit* was crated for transport on the deck of the USS *Memphis*, a cruiser that President Calvin Coolidge sent to bring Lindbergh home. Commissioned as Colonel Charles Lindbergh, he faced frenzied adulation in America as New Yorkers lined Broadway for the tickertape parade honoring the country's hero. The *New York Times* offered $125,000 for Lindbergh's story and an additional $50,000 for a goodwill tour, but money had never been his motive. A memoirist of the 1920s, Frederick Lewis Allen, remarked that "millions" of Lindbergh's countrymen "took him to their hearts as they had taken no other human being in living memory." The journalist Walter Lippmann wrote that Lindbergh transformed "the mundane world with young beauty and unsullied faith."

Two years after the momentous flight, Charles Lindbergh was to marry Anne Morrow (b. 1906), daughter of the US ambassador to Mexico, following a courtship by letters and visits the colonel squeezed into his demanding schedule. On May 27, 1929, the couple were wed at the bride's New Jersey family home, and a honeymoon followed on a motor cruiser on the Long Island Sound. Charles and Anne enjoyed fruit punch at their wedding reception and drank ginger ale while afloat on the Sound. In speakeasies and nightclubs, however, tipplers ordered the cocktail that honored the flyer and the flight.

Lindbergh's solo journey from New York to Paris marked the beginning of the aviation industry. He was soon to scout for Pan American

Airways, founded by visionary entrepreneur Juan Trippe (b. 1899), which launched its first flight, from Key West to Havana, in October 1927. On their joint round-the-world flights, Anne, an accomplished writer and a licensed pilot, flew in the seat behind Charles, operated the radio equipment, and sometimes took the controls of a plane that was outfitted with pontoons for maximally accessible landings on water. Her memoir of their 1931 flight over the Arctic, *North to the Orient*, recounts "twelve hours, by the midnight sun ... over those gray wastes ... isolated and wild as the moon."

Following Pan Am's lead, TWA (Trans World Airlines), which flew Ford trimotor aircraft across the continental US, became a storied name in aviation from its beginnings in 1930. Eastern Air Lines' major route ran between New York and Florida, while smaller airlines, such as Chalk's Flying Service, founded by Arthur ("Pappy") Chalk, a WWI flyer, launched flights between Florida and the Bahamas as early as 1919. While Prohibition commissioner John F. Kramer proclaimed that no liquor would be "hauled . . . in the air" during Prohibition, Chalk smuggled alcohol from the Bahamas to the mainland, and a drink paid homage to the effort.

"Aviation caught me," Amelia Earhart quipped, recalling her childhood yearning to take wing ("I watch the birds flying all day long / And I want to fly too"), especially when powerful, streamlined planes could soar at altitudes of over ten thousand feet. Financial straits, parental discord, and other circumstances in the earlier 1920s delayed Earhart's aeronautic career for several years. A parental breakup and erratic schooling at a finishing school, at the University of Southern California, and then at Columbia University led to a stint as a social worker in the Boston area. Earning a living, Amelia determined to buy a plane, flew in a "Powder Puff Derby" (a label she loathed), gained public attention, and soon promoted commercial aviation as vice president for an East Coast airline. By 1928, she too was a public figure in US aviation.

In June 1928, she planned to fly across the Atlantic Ocean in the Fokker trimotor *Friendship* with WWI flyer Wilmer (Bill) Stultz aboard. Though a superb pilot, Stultz often flew when hungover or "tight," a state Amelia recognized from her father's own "drinking stretches." Believing that Stultz would stay sober in the confines of a cockpit, Amelia overcame her doubts as Stultz alternated with Louis Gordon at the controls, an arrangement Amelia approved after considerable hesitation. A licensed transport pilot, she flew as a passenger, the first woman to cross the Atlantic by air, ready to take over at any minute and doubtless eyeing Stultz until the plane landed safely in south Wales.

One year later, in July 1929, Bill Stultz crashed at Roosevelt Field, Long Island, stunting while drunk and killing himself, at age twenty-nine, along with his two passengers, an event captured in the innovative fiction of John Dos Passos (b. 1896), who would chronicle the era by combining newspaper headlines, biographies, and the lives of fictional characters. In *The Big Money* (1933), readers follow an alcoholic WWI ace named Charley Anderson from a promising career in the 1920s aircraft industry to alcoholic ruin. In the critically acclaimed novel, Prohibition proves no barrier as the former ace travels the country, fueled on gin, scotch, rye, ale, "scotch and soda," and cocktails dubbed "oldfashioneds." The fictional Charley dies when he races an automobile while intoxicated across the track of an oncoming train in Florida, just as Stultz died stunting over rooftops on Long Island.

In 1931, Earhart herself set a world altitude record of 18,415 feet. The tousle-haired, lithe, celebrated "tomboy" flew "the Lindbergh trail" over the North Atlantic in a Lockheed Vega on May 20–21, 1932, landing near Londonderry, Ireland, to become the first woman pilot to fly the route, solo and nonstop.

Four years had passed since the repeal of the Eighteenth Amendment when Earhart embarked on her final flight, a planned round-the-world tour in a Lockheed Electra plane, accompanied by navigator Fred Noonan. Their plane was lost, presumably in a fatal crash, after losing radio contact over the Pacific on July 2, 1937. Unsuccessful searches for the wreckage have spanned decades, and theories about where the plane went down—and why—continue to this day.

During her heyday, Amelia Earhart endorsed a fashion line and, in an unfortunately ill-advised venture, a matched luggage line was later branded under her famous name. Alas, no Prohibition cocktail was dubbed "The Amelia," but the Aviation honors the "Queen of the Air." For his part, Lucky Lindy's fortunes took a dark turn in later years with the murder and kidnapping of his infant son and the suspicion that he harbored Nazi sympathies on the eve of the Second World War.

THE ASBACH COCKTAIL

Ingredients

1. 1–2 ounces Asbach brandy
2. 3–4 ounces soda water
3. Lemon twist

Directions

1. In highball glass, add cubed ice to taste.
2. Add brandy.
3. Add soda.
4. Squeeze and add lemon twist, stir, and serve.

SCOTCH AND SODA

Ingredients

1. 1–2 ounces scotch whisky
2. Chilled soda water
3. Cubed ice

Directions

1. In highball glass, add ice.
2. Add whisky.
3. Top with soda and stir gently.

OLD FASHION(ED)

Ingredients

1. 1–2 ounces rye or bourbon whiskey
2. 1 dash Angostura bitters
3. Small lump sugar
4. Half slice orange
5. Large piece of ice

Directions

1. Place sugar in small tumbler.
2. Add dash of bitters onto sugar lump.
3. Add enough water to dissolve sugar.
4. Add whiskey and ice.
5. Stir, add orange slice, and serve.

LINDBERGH CROSSING

Ingredients

1. 2 ounces cognac
2. ½ ounce Bénédictine
3. ½ ounce fresh lime juice
4. Lime slice for garnish

Directions

1. Pour first three ingredients into chilled glass.
2. Add cubed ice.
3. Stir carefully.
4. When drink is maximally cold, garnish with lime slice.

"PAPPY" CHALK

Ingredients

1. ½ ounce dark rum
2. 1 ounce Swedish punsch
3. ½ ounce Cocchi Americano
4. ½ ounce fresh lime juice
5. Lime slice for garnish

Directions

1. Add first four ingredients to mixing glass.
2. Add goodly amount of cubed ice.
3. Stir carefully until drink is maximally cold.
4. Strain into chilled glass and garnish with lime slice.

THE AVIATION COCKTAIL

Ingredients

1. 1½ ounces Plymouth gin
2. ¾ ounce fresh lemon juice
3. 1 teaspoon crème de violette
4. 1 teaspoon maraschino liqueur
5. Maraschino cherry for garnish

Directions

1. Add first four ingredients to mixing glass.
2. Add goodly amount of cubed ice.
3. Stir carefully until drink is maximally chilled.
4. Add garnish.

HARRY'S NEW YORK BAR, PARIS

After the Great War, Harry MacElhone, a Scotsman who had tended bar at Ciro's in London, crossed the Channel to take up residence in Paris at the New York Bar, a converted bistro at number 5 Rue Daunou, between the Rue de la Paix and the Avenue de l'Opéra. Owned since 1911 by an American jockey, Ted Sloan, and a partner named Clancy, the place was renamed Harry's New York Bar when MacElhone bought it in 1923, expecting his enterprise to be a sure-shot draw for homesick American tourists and expatriates. There, MacElhone is credited for inventing several drinks, including the White Lady, the Bloody Mary, and the Boulevardiere (reportedly a favorite of Ernest Hemingway's). In 1924, the *Chicago Tribune* reported that the winning entry in a contest for the best name for "the lawless drinker of illegally made or illegally obtained liquor" to be the brand new word "scofflaw" (one who flouts and scoffs at the law) and "reported that Harry's bar in Paris had invented the Scofflaw cocktail, which was 'exceedingly popular among American prohibition dodgers.'"

The bar also became the favorite watering hole of foreign corre-spondents, and the novelist Sinclair Lewis tapped his own early years in newspaper work to fictionalize the bar in his novel *Dodsworth* (1928). In the story, a retired auto executive, Sam Dodsworth, tours Europe for the first time with Fran, his wife of many years, and the couple's estrangement reveals itself as they sojourn in London and Paris. Mrs. Dodsworth gravitates to the Parisian *artistes* her hus-band suspects are pretentious phonies, while Sam longs for the "low and intelligent company" to be found at the New York Bar, where he is acquainted with a dozen journalists. He yearns for their "com-monplace shop-talk: how Trotsky really got along with Stalin . . . what was the 'low-down' on the international battle of oil." Sam also hears the well-informed newspaper reporter's lament, that he'll be judged "pedantic" unless he sounds "like a longshoreman." In the bar one afternoon, the reporters discuss politics and automobiles with Sam. Buoyed by the shoptalk, he returns to the hotel to find his wife dressing for an evening at the theater. Her greeting to Sam: "You smell of whisky! Atrociously!"

Harry's New York Bar, free of Prohibition's US constraints, served whiskies and mixed drinks of unimpeachable quality, and Harry MacElhone authored two invaluable books for bartenders on both sides of the Pond: *Barflies and Cocktails* (1927) and *ABC of Mixing Cocktails* (1930).

BOULEVARDIERE COCKTAIL

Ingredients

1. 1 ounce bourbon whiskey
2. 1 ounce Campari
3. 1 ounce sweet vermouth
4. Maraschino cherry

Directions

1. In mixing glass with ice, add first three ingredients.
2. Stir well.
3. Strain into cocktail glass.
4. Garnish with maraschino cherry.

SCOFFLAW COCKTAIL

Ingredients

1. 1½ ounces Canadian Club whiskey
2. 1½ ounces French vermouth
3. ½ ounce grenadine
4. ½ ounce lemon juice
5. 1 dash orange bitters

Directions

1. In shaker with cubed ice, add all ingredients.
2. Shake vigorously.
3. Strain and serve in cocktail glass.

JOURNALIST COCKTAIL

Ingredients

1. 2 ounces gin
2. ½ ounce Italian vermouth
3. ½ ounce French vermouth
4. 2 dashes curaçao
5. 1 dash Angostura bitters

Directions

1. In shaker filled with ice, add all ingredients.
2. Shake vigorously.
3. Strain and serve in cocktail glass.

FOREIGN CORRESPONDENT COCKTAIL

Ingredients

1. 1 ounce calvados
2. ½ ounce Bénédictine
3. ½ ounce lime juice
4. Lime slice for garnish

Directions

1. Put first three ingredients in mixing glass.
2. Add ample ice.
3. Stir gently.
4. Strain into cocktail glass and garnish with lime slice.

HARRY MACELHONE'S 1920S PARIS RECIPE

Ingredients

1. 1½ ounces applejack or calvados
2. ¾ ounce dry gin
3. ¾ ounce orange juice
4. ¾ ounce fresh lemon or lime juice
5. ½ ounce French vermouth
6. ½ ounce Italian vermouth
7. Grenadine to color (½ ounce)

Directions

1. Put all ingredients into shaker.
2. Add ample ice and shake vigorously.
3. Strain into cocktail glass.
4. Garnish with lime or lemon twist.

THE SILVER SCREEN

"Go to a motion picture ... and let yourself go," coaxed the advertisement in the *Saturday Evening Post*. For the price of a ticket and a free afternoon or evening, "a wonderful new world" awaited with "all the adventure, all the romance, all the excitement" to be found in a Spanish ranchero in *The Mark of Zorro* (1920), an Arabian Nights fable in *The Thief of Baghdad* (1925), or the musical drama of *The Jazz Singer* (1927). Exotic worlds beckoned at the local bijou theater or a sumptuous movie palace in the heart of the city. From silent films to the "talkies," the decade of the 1920s capped a quarter-century of motion picture advances that gave America a singular sensation captured in one word: pictures!

The public first glimpsed motion pictures at the 1893 World's Columbian Exposition in Chicago, an international fair where an Edison machine, the Kinetoscope, offered ninety seconds of tiny, two-dimensional humans in motion. The miniature black-and-white figures struck viewers as remote and alien, no relation to the vibrant vaudeville performers onstage in a theater. As the new century approached, twenty-minute programs flickered in arcades to become profitable novelties, especially when films were deliberately slowed down, speeded up, or run backward. Cars zipped down the street in reverse, and swimmers sprang out of the water, feet first, to regain footing on dry land. The nickelodeons' humorous stunts flourished in working-class neighborhoods when a five-cent piece, often needed for a soup bone or lamp oil, could be spared for entertainment.

The cusp of the twentieth century pulsed with skills that set the stage for "movie-made America," according to film historian Robert Sklar, who tallied the photographers, electrical workers, writers, editors, directors, costume designers, and others, including persons skillful in applying cosmetics or casting performers. New York briefly bid to become the center of film production, but Southern California's year-round sunshine, mild climate, and expanses of wide-open space won out, especially as nearby terrain varied from desert to mountains. Over four thousand acres of Los Angeles's Griffith Park could become the Wild West, the Mojave, the desert of Arabia, or the Grand Canyon. By the mid-1910s, the name of the Los Angeles area known as Hollywood had become shorthand for the movie industry and filmdom's expansive culture.

The short films relied, at first, on motion that mimicked carnival acts (acrobats, boxing cats, a contortionist) or tapped a humorous vein from daily life, such as fun in a barroom (Prohibition two decades into the future). Large-screen projection, however, inspired awe when viewers gazed at scenes never before captured on the screen: "crashing waves, onrushing locomotives, the wonders of nature." The luminescent projection screens, embedded with highly reflective aluminum or silver, made the "silver screen" a catchphrase for movies.

For longer films, producers snagged storylines from novels, such as Upton Sinclair's *The Jungle* or Victor Hugo's *The Hunchback of*

Notre Dame. Historical events were ripe for film, as were fairy tales and episodes from the Bible: the Easter story in *The Passion Play*; a young boy chased by a giant in *Jack and the Beanstalk*; wartime reenactments in *Shooting Captured Insurgents, Spanish-American War.* In one film, *The Execution of Mary, Queen of Scots,* the axe beheaded a realistic dummy, while Mary was played by a man. Eros proved irresistible, with come-on titles promising screens filled with women in *dishabille.* The 1903 roster included *The Corset Model, The Physical Culture Girl,* and *From Showgirl to Burlesque Queen.* That year, kissing and caressing were featured at length in *Be Good* and *The Girl at the Window.*

Film devotees agree that an early cinematic milestone was *The Great Train Robbery* (1903), a suspenseful action-packed Western, with an office safe blown open on a moving train, bandits balancing atop the cars, and a dramatic final shoot-out with its *pièce de résistance*: a scowling, bearded bandit who faces the audience, then fires a revolver at the viewer, point blank. Audiences cringed and ducked at the surprising finale, and the film toured the country, a spectacular success to be widely imitated in years to come. A dozen years later, in 1915, white audiences thrilled to D. W. Griffith's *The Birth of a Nation,* set in the post–Civil War Reconstruction era and adapted from the racist novel *The Klansman,* by Thomas Dixon, Jr. The film portrays Lincoln's death as inspiration for the Ku Klux Klan's cavalry charge on a Southern town where the white citizenry endures African American rule. Black citizens organized to ban the film, which was nonetheless praised for skillful continuity and epic battle scenes. With a soundtrack of Richard Wagner's "The Ride of the Valkyries," *The Birth of a Nation* was termed "the eighth wonder of the world."

As the industry grew, movie moguls, their names familiar to this day, emerged to head new businesses that produced and distributed films, often in theaters their companies owned: Adolph Zukor, William Fox, the Warner brothers (Harry, Albert, Samuel, and Jack, who were, at birth, the Wonskolaser brothers). In a pioneering business, these first- and second-generation Jews from Central and Eastern Europe faced less of the entrenched anti-Semitism common in American business and the professions. Entrepreneurs of the new mass media, they took command. By 1928, the US boasted twenty-eight thousand theaters, roughly half of them located in or near urban centers (one theater seat for every five to seven men, women, and children in the country).

Common sense dictated that film roles would be filled by stage performers from vaudeville, Broadway, or touring companies, but acting on film sets and locations proved radically different from live theater, and few stage actors successfully crossed that Rubicon. For thespians of the stage, the absence of energizing live audiences deflated energy and ruined timing. Film scenes, what's more, were often shot in seemingly random succession, with the actors called upon to work in a back-to-back jumble of peace, war, rage, sorrow, love, and so on. The elaborate, exaggerated pantomime fundamental to the successful silent films also proved daunting for actors whose stagecraft ill-suited the popular new medium. Dorothy Gish (b. 1898), the younger sister of the better-known Lillian Gish, transitioned from the stage to movie bit parts and, finally, to five-reel productions, notably *Old Heidelberg* and *Jordan Is a Hard Road*. Her light comedy marked a stark contrast to the sultry Theda Bara (b. 1885), an early sex symbol of the silver screen who starred in (and as) *Cleopatra* and *Salomé*, and as *An Unchastened Woman*, among other films that cast her as a vamp (and a vampire too). The Gish sisters and Theda Bara starred in silent films, but the talkies featured actors whose voices projected dramatically, among them the Hungarian-born Bela Lugosi (b. 1882), a WWI veteran who found fame in such horror films as *Dracula* and *White Zombie* in the early 1930s, just before Prohibition ended.

Two performers succeeded especially brilliantly when trading the stage for the movie lot, both to win public acclaim, flex business muscles, and earn sums unimaginable for stage actors. Douglas Fairbanks (b. 1883) and Mary Pickford (b. 1892), film stars of the first magnitude by 1920, had been child actors who toured with traveling troupes, Fairbanks mainly in the West, Pickford from her native Toronto. (The necessity of salable names recast Douglas Ullman as Fairbanks, while Gladys Louise Smith became Mary Pickford.)

The public stormed the box office to view the dashing, swashbuckling Fairbanks in *Robin Hood*, *The Thief of Baghdad*, or *The Mark of Zorro*, just as they clamored for the next picture starring "America's Sweetheart," Mary Pickford, who starred in *The Poor Little Rich Girl*, *Rebecca of Sunnybrooke Farm*, *Rosita*, *Little Annie Rooney*, *Coquette*, and a dazzling range of other reels. (Said Pickford, "I played scrubwomen and secretaries and women of all nationalities. . . . I decided that if I could, I'd get into as many pictures as possible.") Though the "talkies" curtailed her film career, the beloved Pickford, a multimillionaire with an estate named "Pickfair," shed stardust to promote women's suffrage. During Prohibition, she climbed onto the nose of a new Ford trimotor airplane, the *City of Los Angeles*, to christen the aircraft with a bottle of grape juice. Mary Pickford and Douglas Fairbanks divorced their first spouses to wed one another in 1920, the year Prohibition began.

While the slapstick Keystone Kops clownishly amused audiences, throughout the 1920s a mustached Charlie Chaplin (b. 1889) donned a frockcoat with a shirt and tie, baggy trousers, oversize shoes, a cane, and a bowler hat to become a screen icon, the Little Tramp, who debuted in a silent film of 1915, *The Tramp*, and thereafter soared to popularity in silent films inflected with social issues, such as immigration and poverty,

often with sweetened endings. Magazines devoted to movies and movie stars, especially *Photoplay*, spotlighted the British-born Chaplin and self-styled intellectuals, notably Gilbert Seldes, wrote at length about his social and cultural significance. "What makes Chaplin great," intoned Seldes in *The Seven Lively Arts* (1924), "is that he has irony and pity . . . both piety and wit." Chaplin went on to produce and direct films well into the twentieth century, but the Little Tramp endures as a classic of the Roaring Twenties, ranging from *The Kid* (1921) to *The Pilgrim* (1923) and *The Gold Rush* (1925), in which the hungover Little Tramp "cooks and eats his boots, devouring the shoelaces as if they were spaghetti." At the first Academy Awards ceremony in May 1929, Chaplin won an honorary award for acting, writing, directing, and producing.

Filmdom demanded glamor, the two terms signifying ultraluxurious lives onscreen and off, for Hollywood homes of the Jazz Age tasked architects to dream big—and biggest. The hills and canyons of greater Los Angeles boasted Rudolph Valentino's "Falcon's Lair," Cecil B. DeMille's "Paradise," and others built like film fantasies of Mediterranean villas, Tudor castles, Swiss chalets, Egyptian temples. Their swimming pools, ballrooms, pipe organs, and wine cellars stocked with rare vintages made each star's and mogul's home a personal Shangri-La. Their projection rooms, palatial bathrooms, sunken tubs, and gold fixtures all suggested that vast wealth was the key to fulfillment in America.

The stars' palatial seclusion briefly ceased for the pageantry of world premieres as the movements of movie royalty outshone the coronations of kings and queens. Searchlights scanned the heavens and stars paraded into a palatial theater "lined with crimson velvet and marble," the walls adorned with paintings, the lobby filled with uniformed ushers for the screening of a film that was soon to be shown to all America and the world at large. The novelist and social critic Upton Sinclair found himself drawn to such a scene in *Oil!* (1927), a novel that stretched its canvas from petroleum industry scandals to the manners and mores of Hollywood. On the afternoon of a premiere, wrote Sinclair, "crowds pack the streets," and "the police department is required to make pathway for the movie stars as they move in their appointed courses, from the shining ten thousand dollar limousines . . . through the arcade and under the million dollar portals." As they move, "a dozen motion picture cameras grind, and flash-lights boom, and the crowd surges and quivers and murmurs with ecstasy. . . . The crowd surges, and rushes wildly, and women faint, and ambulances come clanging."

Hollywood chafed to bring cocktails to the silver screen, and filmdom got its wish in 1934, the year following Prohibition's repeal, when the first of the six *Thin Man* movies debuted, starring Myrna Loy and William Powell as the stylish, sophisticated private detectives Nick and Nora Charles. The two have been dubbed "the first and most famous duo of drinkers," who held "a beverage in hand in every other scene." Nick and Nora favored the Bronx cocktail, while the gin-and-champagne French 75, a favorite since its appearance in the *Savoy Cocktail Book* (1930), was served to Rick and Ilsa (Humphrey Bogart and Ingrid Bergman) in *Casablanca*. Not to be outdone in its cocktail selection, the 1959 Hitchcock classic *North by Northwest* starred Cary Grant and Eva Marie Saint, who flirted on a train over a Gibson (a Martini with an onion instead of an olive). And so it went, on to moviedom's James Bond, secret agent 007, whose Martinis must forever be "shaken, not stirred." The Prohibition years had shaken and stirred the country, but the stars have, ever after, freely raised their glasses on the silver screen.

FAIRBANKS COCKTAIL

Ingredients

1. 2 ounces gin
2. 1 ounce French vermouth
3. 2 dashes orange bitters
4. 2 dashes crème de noyaux

Directions

1. In chilled mixing glass, add gin and vermouth.
2. Add ice.
3. Add bitters and crème de noyaux.
4. Stir, strain, and serve in cocktail glass.

MARY PICKFORD COCKTAIL

Ingredients

1. 2 ounces white rum
2. 1 teaspoon grenadine

3. 1¾ ounces fresh pineapple juice
4. ½ teaspoon maraschino liqueur
5. Maraschino cherry

Directions

1. In cocktail shaker, add rum.
2. Add pineapple juice, grenadine, and maraschino liqueur.
3. Add ice, shake, strain into cocktail glass.
4. Garnish with maraschino cherry and serve.

CHARLIE CHAPLIN COCKTAIL

Ingredients

1. 1 ounce fresh lime juice
2. 1 ounce sloe gin
3. 1 ounce apricot brandy
4. Ice

Directions

1. Add lime juice, gin, and brandy to cocktail shaker.
2. Fill shaker with ice.
3. Shake well, strain, and serve in cocktail glass.

DOROTHY GISH COCKTAIL

Ingredients

1. 2 ounces rum
2. ¼ ounce apricot brandy
3. ½ ounce orange juice
4. ½ ounce fresh pineapple juice

Directions

1. In cocktail shaker, add rum, brandy, and juices.
2. Add ample ice to shaker.
3. Shake vigorously, strain into chilled cocktail glass, and serve.

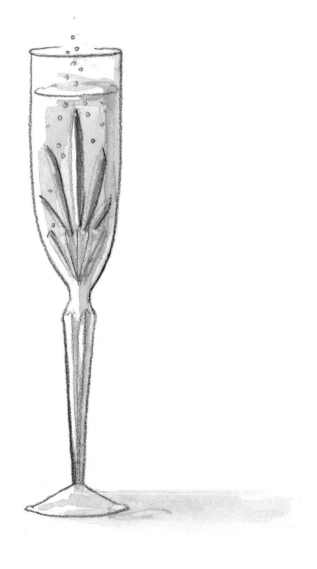

THEDA BARA COCKTAIL

Ingredients

1. 2 ounces Plymouth gin
2. 1 ounce dry vermouth
3. ½ ounce triple sec
4. 1 ounce pomegranate juice
5. 1 ounce pomegranate syrup (optional)
6. 1 dash orange bitters

Directions

1. In chilled mixing glass, add ingredients in order.
2. Add ample ice cubes.
3. Stir thoroughly.
4. Strain into tall glass filled with ice and serve.

BELA LUGOSI COCKTAIL

Ingredients

1. 1½ ounces rye whiskey
2. 1 ounce Dubonnet
3. 1½ ounces triple sec
4. 3 dashes orange bitters
5. Orange peel twist for garnish

Directions

1. In chilled mixing glass, add ingredients except for orange peel.
2. Add ample ice cubes.
3. Stir gently but thoroughly.
4. Strain into cocktail glass, add garnish, and serve.

A "DRY" CHRISTMAS

America's fabled Yuletide past seems traceable to Charles Dickens's heartwarming *A Christmas Carol* (1843) and Clement C. Moore's *A Visit from St. Nicholas* (1820), better known as "The Night Before Christmas." The historian Karal Ann Marling, however, pinpoints the origin of America's "Olde Fashioned" Christmas in *The Sketch-Book of Geoffrey Crayon* (1820), by Washington Irving. A founding figure in American literature, Irving staged scenes of holiday merriment in his fictional Bracebridge Hall, where Christmas revels meant roasted meats, "Dame Mince pie, storytelling, Mistletoe," and physical games of "hot cockles," involving kicks to the buttocks of a player whose head was buried in someone's lap.

Christmas, American style, had long foundered on debates about etiquette and custom—whether or not Santa ought to be slender or roly-poly, fully bearded or fringed with whiskers, or whether a fir tree strung with Edison's electrical lights instead of candles could inspire carolers' "O Tannenbaum." Should gifts be presented in plain sight or hidden in ornate wrapping papers and tied with ribbons and bows? For decades, department store show windows had sparked the Christmas spirit with Santas and Lilliputian scenes of his North Pole workshop.

The 1920s stepped it all up. In Philadelphia, Gimbel Brothers Department Store sponsored "the official arrival of Santa Claus" in a parade featuring a fireman dressed as St. Nicholas, while New York's Macy's Christmas Parade was launched in 1924, with horse-drawn floats, bands, and animals from the Central Park Zoo, including elephants, camels, donkeys, and goats. Secular merchandise far outpaced the purchase of religious items in sales, and a Hallmark Christmas card wishes the receiver, "Whatever you want on Christmas Day, I hope you get it." The desired gifts might include "a town-car," a "fur coat," and a "motor boat." (One disgruntled observer believed such materialism was spawned by the "Moscow Society of the Godless.") Though no Hallmark card of Prohibition years featured alcoholic Yuletide cheer, international advertising splashed the verboten bottles on the pages of offshore newspapers and magazines: Seagram's, "the World's Favorites"; Martini & Rossi "For All Your Cocktails"; Gilbey's "Crystal Clear" dry gin; and champagnes galore, not to mention Baccarat crystal ("the perfect cocktail glass") and Christofle barware ("known the world over for the quality of its silverware").

In America, meanwhile, a jovial Santa promoted sweets in solid and liquid form, the sugars unsullied by alcohol. Rotund in his fur-trimmed suit and with eyes twinkling merrily, Santa Claus promoted "Coca-Cola, the pause that refreshes" and Whitman's chocolate candy "for everybody's Christmas." Both were featured in the pages of the popular *Saturday Evening Post* magazine, famed for its covers by artist Norman Rockwell. Whether Santa held a glass of coke aloft in a Yuletide toast or proffered a gift box of chocolates, Americans were never to suspect the cola might be spiked or the centers of the chocolates filled with brandy or rum.

Among the 1920s "plaintiffs" in the case against the "dry" Prohibition was a figure dubbed the Old Soak, an invention of Don Marquis (b. 1878), a humorist and newspaperman whose fiction was mixed with philosophy. Marquis's Old Soak took his place with other folksy, "cracker barrel" philosophers, from Mark Twain's characters to Marquis's contemporary Will Rogers, an Oklahoman who rose to national fame by opining in his own name. The Old Soak appeared in 1921 as Prohibition took hold, a curmudgeonly character who decried "home-made booze" and vowed to depart the US unless "the smuggling trade develops into what it ought to." Indeed it did, but the Christmas season presented its own challenges to one whose name, Old Soak, refers to a man who imbibes most seriously:

"Christmas," said the Old Soak, "will soon be here. But me, I ain't going to look at it. I ain't got the heart to face it. I'm going to crawl off and make arrangements to go to sleep on the twenty-third of December and not wake up until the second of January.

"Them that is in favour of a denaturized Christmas won't be interfered with by me. I got no grudge against them. But I won't intrude any on them, either. They can pass through the holidays in an orgy of sobriety, and I'll be all alone in my own little room, with my memories and a case of Bourbon to bear me up.

"I never could look on Christmas with the naked eye. It makes me so darned sad, Christmas does. There's the kids . . . I used to give 'em presents, and my tendency was to weep as I give them. 'Poor little rascals,' I said to myself, 'they think life is going to be just one Christmas tree after another, but it ain't.' And then I'd think of all the Christmases past I had spent with good friends, and how they was all gone, or on their way. And I'd think of all the poor folks on Christmas, and how the efforts made for them at that season was only a drop in the bucket to what they'd need the year around. And along about December twenty-third I always got so downhearted and sentimental and discouraged about the whole darned universe I nearly died with melancholy.

"In years past, the remedy was at hand. A few drinks and I could look even Christmas in the face. A few more and I'd stand under the mistletoe and sing, 'God rest ye merry, gentlemen.' And by the night of Christmas day I had kidded myself into thinking I liked it, and wanted to keep it up for a week.

"But this Christmas there ain't going to be any general iniquity used to season the grand religious festival with, except among a few of us Old Soaks that has it laid away. I ain't got the heart to look on all the melancholy critters that will be remembering the drinks they had last years. And I ain't going to trot my own feelings out and make 'em public, neither. No sir. Me, I'm going to hibernate like a bear that goes to sleep with his thumb in his mouth. Only it won't be a thumb I have in my mouth. My house will be full of children and grandchildren, and there will be a passel of my wife's relations that has always boosted for Prohibition, but any of 'em ain't going to see the old man. I won't mingle in any of them debilitated festivities. I ain't any Old Scrooge, but I respect the memory of the old-time Christmas, and I'm going to have mind all by myself, the melancholy part of it that comes first, and the cure for the melancholy. This country ain't worthy to share in my kind of a Christmas, and I ain't so much as going to stick my head out of the window and let it smell my breath till after the holidays is over. I got presents for all of 'em, but none of 'em is to be allowed to open the old man's door and poke any presents into his room for him. They ain't worthy to give me presents, the people in general in this country ain't, and I won't take none from them. They might 'a' got together and stopped this Prohibition thing before it got such a start, but they didn't have the gumption. I've seceded, I have. And if any of my wife's Prohibition relations comes sniffin' and smellin' around my door, where I've locked myself in, I'll put a bullet through the door. You hear me! And I'll know who's sniffin', too, for I can tell a Prohibitionist sniff as fur as I can hear it.

"I got a bar of my own all fixed up in my bedroom and there's going to be a hot water kettle near by it and a bowl of this here Tom and Jerry setting onto it as big as life.

"And every time I wake up I'll crawl out of bed and say to myself: 'Better have just one more.'"

The holiday bowl of Tom and Jerry (named for Jerry Thomas, the 1800s bartender who invented the drink he named for himself) ferried the woebegone Old Soak from Christmas into the New Year, so he need not know of master bartender Frank Meier of the Ritz Bar, Paris, who offered two recipes for Christmas punch in *The Artistry of Mixing Drinks* (1936). First published in a limited edition of three hundred copies, Meier's compendium provided a cold punch and a hot one. In the spirit of winter, here is Meier's recipe for a large-scale wassail:

CHRISTMAS PUNCH HOT

Ingredients
1. 2 bottles brandy (@ 25.4 ounces per bottle)
2. 2 bottles champagne (@ 25.4 ounces per bottle)
3. 1 pound sugar
4. 1 pound fresh pineapple, cubed and crushed

Directions
1. In gallon saucepan (or larger), pour brandy (reserve 3–4 ounces).
2. Pour in champagne.
3. Add sugar.
4. Add pineapple.
5. Heat until the mixture foams, but do not boil.
6. Pour reserved brandy on top, set aflame, allow to burn for one minute.
7. Serve each drink in heated wineglass with spoon (serves twenty-five to thirty).

IN THE MONEY (While It Lasts)

A popular 1920s tune, "My God, How the Money Rolls In," suited the mood of a soaring stock market and money-mad America. The brief post-WWI years of frightening unemployment and raging inflation had inspired a business adage of 1921: "money rewards the exercise of keen brains and quick wits." Two years later, the downturn years seemed a mere hiccup, and Americans felt deservedly flush. Steady employment provided money for more leisure, enjoyment, and consumption, and Wall Street's booming stocks augured a future of endless dividends. The tickertape proved "free" money was perpetually on the rise, easily available from brokers who sold stocks on the slimmest of margins. Hit songs—"Blue Skies" and "My Blue Heaven"—reflected the celestial temper of the times.

Citizens as investors and consumers were energized by advertising that was cleverly refashioned by public relations guru Edward Bernays (b. 1891), a nephew of Sigmund Freud. Advertising had

flourished from the late 1800s through the 1910s, when magazines and street signage hailed superior products from shoe polish to hats. As the 1920s advanced, the ads pivoted from extolling the attributes of the products they featured to consumers' experience of happiness and exhilaration, instilling faith in consumption as near-term nirvana. Purchases insured well-being and higher status, while credit offices eased the way with installment buying "on time" with "easy" payment plans. If debt mounted, no matter. Tomorrow would take care of itself.

Hand in glove with creditors, corporations often set strict, high sales quotas, and retail clerks and salesmen honed high-pressure tactics. Recalled a Ford dealer in 1927, "You do a lot of things when someone is riding you that you wouldn't do under ordinary circumstances. . . .

If Mr. Ford knew personally some of the things that go on, I am sure he would call a halt to his branch managers riding the local agents the way they do." The dealer, mindful of a car repossessed for late payments, had lost track of the customer: "The last I heard of him, he was bootlegging."

Fords and Chevrolets, new or second-hand, gassed up to hit the road to seek fortunes from the 1920s Florida land boom. Entrepreneurs Henry M. Flagler and Henry B. Plant had stitched Florida with railroads and built vacation hotels in the 1890s, and the immensely wealthy Flagler built a bold rail line, completed in 1912, stretching over islands and ocean channels from Miami to Key West. A decade later, automobiles were routed along the new eighteen-foot-wide Dixie Highway, a main artery down the East Coast, soon to be dubbed US 1 and already luring families to Florida, especially under the influence of Midwest hometown newspaper propaganda touting riches for first-time investors that paralleled Wall Street's "invincible" bull market. With tales of alligators and Seminole Indian wars consigned to boys' adventure books, novice speculators prepared to pounce. Many would fall prey to dubious schemes.

One journalist, Gertrude Mathews Shelby, a neophyte "investor," recounted her roller-coaster ride in "Florida Frenzy," published in the January 1926 issue of *Harper's Monthly Magazine*. Beware of the "free" trips, dinners, and airplane rides meant to whet appetites for properties, she warned. The house lots outlined on maps in the "realty magicians'" offices might be actually under water, or in a sinkhole. She would know.

Gertrude counted herself among "the credulous millions who would buy lots from plats without even visiting the land!" "It doesn't matter what the price is," she was told, "if the location is where the buyer is lively." The schemes relied on "paper profits" that multiplied exponentially from buyers' initial deposits. "The next man assumes your obligation," cooed Gertrude's salesman. "You ride on his money. He passes the buck to somebody else if he can. . . . It's not so hazardous as it sounds." Gertrude had snapped up the "bargain" of a fifty-foot lot offered at $1,000 by a supposedly "reputable firm." The result: "the bonanza turned out to be . . . a rockpit."

In years to come, the deeds to Florida wetlands proved as worthless as many Wall Street stocks, especially when the 1930s Depression made the twenties feel like a fever dream. In the meantime, as the 1921 song went, "Ain't We Got Fun?" Fun it was for folks who had long lived in modest circumstances but now felt socially "high hat" and financially "in clover." (Eighty percent of Americans had no savings in the years leading to the crash of 1929.) The "quick wealth tales" "multiplied astoundingly" and "pyramided high into the thousands."

For all her efforts, Gertrude managed one $13,000 windfall from a "flipped" property. For others, however, the Florida land boom was ruinous.

MILLIONAIRE COCKTAIL

Ingredients

1. ½ ounce dark rum
2. ½ ounce sloe gin
3. ½ ounce apricot brandy
4. ½ ounce lime juice
5. ½ teaspoon grenadine

Directions

1. Put ingredients in mixing glass.
2. Add ample ice.
3. Stir gently, strain, and serve.

RICH DADDY

Ingredients

1. 1½ ounces applejack or calvados
2. ½ ounce Cocchi Americano
3. 1 teaspoon clove syrup
4. Lemon peel twist for garnish

Directions

1. Put first three ingredients into mixing glass.
2. Add ample ice.
3. Stir gently and strain into Old Fashioned glass filled with ice.
4. Garnish with lemon twist.

HIGH HAT

Ingredients

1. 1 ounce applejack or calvados
2. ½ ounce Swedish punsch
3. ½ ounce Campari
4. Orange peel twist to garnish

Directions

1. Put first three ingredients into mixing glass.
2. Add ample ice and stir gently.
3. Strain into Old Fashioned glass filled with ice.
4. Garnish with orange peel twist.

BURIED IN CLOVER

Ingredients

1. 2¼ ounces Canadian whisky
2. 2 teaspoons clove syrup
3. 1 dash Angostura bitters
4. Orange slice studded with cloves for garnish

Directions

1. Put whisky and syrup into mixing glass.
2. Add ample ice and stir gently.
3. Strain into Old Fashioned glass filled with ice.
4. Add bitters and garnish.

THE PARTY'S OVER

I say to you, that from this date on, the Eighteenth Amendment
is doomed!

—Franklin Delano Roosevelt, Democratic Convention, 1932

From the late 1920s, the Volstead Act's "doom" became a gambler's wager on *when* and *how* repeal would officially take place, rather than *if*. Mounting pressure for repeal intensified, and voices swelled to a chorus. Business leaders objected to the unworkable law, as did medical societies and bar associations. Citizens' groups chimed in to urge repeal, including the Women's Organization for National Prohibition Reform. Organized brewers and distillers, exiled into a decade-long "wilderness," likewise rallied to the cause. Sensing their mission's imminent collapse, prohibitionists prophesized disaster with the return of saloons. Nevertheless, the tide had turned against the "drys" and their "noble experiment."

None of the alcohol amply consumed during this period had been subject to taxation, and the depleted US Treasury in the post-1929 Depression years cried out for funds. President Franklin D. Roosevelt, inaugurated in 1933, promptly issued executive orders that severely reduced the enforcement budgets, and Congress passed a resolution that

submitted a repeal amendment to state conventions. State by state, the Twenty-First Amendment to repeal the Eighteenth was passed, with Utah beating Maine as the thirty-sixth and final state needed to end Prohibition (the only constitutional amendment in US history to be repealed). Quipped historian Herbert Asbury, "It was the depression which finally broke the back of the dry camel."

The ebullient "drys" of the temperance movement evidently had forgotten Abraham Lincoln's famous admonition: with "public support, nothing can fail," but "without it, nothing can succeed." The failed "noble experiment" finally came to an end on December 5, 1933. Looking back a half-century later, *Vogue's* Diana Vreeland remarked, "It's hard to believe now that Prohibition ever existed—it seems like a fairy tale." In his famous *ABC of Mixing Cocktails*, renowned bartender Harry MacElhone had included an effervescent tonic that promised relief from indigestion and hangovers. "A good pick-me-up for that next morning feeling," he wrote. His words may aptly describe the "hangover" of Prohibition:

THE BROMO-SELTZER

Ingredients

1. Bromo-Seltzer
2. Soda water

Directions

1. Put 1 tablespoon of Bromo-Seltzer in tumbler.
2. Fill with soda.
3. Pour into a second tumbler.
4. Repeat twice until powder is dissolved.
5. Drink while fizzing.

ACKNOWLEDGMENTS

This project arose from a strong suspicion that my grandmother, a wholesale baker in Pittsburgh, Pennsylvania, had been a bootlegger's girlfriend during Prohibition. For decades, the Nicholas Bakery at 619 Homewood Avenue had supplied snack foods to the city's taverns, country clubs, and nightclubs in a distribution network covering metropolitan "Steel City" Pittsburgh. From the end of WWII into the early 1950s, when I knew her, "Nana" rose before dawn to "fix" her upswept gray-blonde hair, apply makeup, slip on her stockings and suede pumps, add pearl earrings, and tie a baker's apron over her dress to toil mightily, with helpers, to produce hundreds of dozens of oatmeal and peanut butter cookies, plus slices of pound cake and jellyroll, all cellophane wrapped into snack packs by deft-fingered Ann and Maude in the afternoons as a radio broadcast soap operas: *The Romance of Helen Trent, Ma Perkins, As the World Turns.*

In those years, the Nicholas Bakery still had the Wise Potato Chip and Bachman Pretzel franchises—all operated from "the shop," a gray clapboard, barnlike building in an alley off the avenue. Delivery trucks made the rounds, from taverns to the nightclubs that had outlasted their Prohibition years, like Bill Green's and Jackie Heller's Carousel.

Nana's Prohibition years, from the 1920s to 1933, came my way in hints: the closetful of aging furs (sealskin coats, chinchilla, mink), the cascades of pearl and diamond jewelry, the reverential references to the mysterious "Mister Nicholas" and his Packard automobile, and especially the story of a police chase with handguns firing, an indelible memory. (If only my elementary school self had the wit to record the details!)

Once again, I pop a cork for literary agent Deirdre Mullane, who suggested this second volume of US social history told through its cocktail menu. *Jazz Age Cocktails* follows *Gilded Age Cocktails*, a sequence appreciated by Clara Platter, senior editor at New York University Press, who once again ferried a "cocktail" proposal into a formal plan and put the book into the expert team at the Press, including manager Martin Coleman and editor Dan Geist, together with Mary Beth Jarrad. The superb design of this volume is credited to Charles Boyd Hames, who "sculpted" the interior, and to Adam Bohannon, who fashioned the elegantly "jazzy" cover. Good friends, specialists in their fields of research, generously responded to my queries about reliable 1920s research sources, and this book benefits from Mark Cirino's expertise on Hemingway, Jennifer Fay's on the early US cinema, and Thadious Davis's knowledge of the Harlem Renaissance, which brought a satchel of sources from her library to my front door.

Jazz Age Cocktails benefits greatly from the focused attention of outside reviewers who have combined critique with appreciation. Their meticulous attention to the project has sharpened its content, heartened this author, and opened a conversation we might all enjoy over a cocktail. This project has also been built from the many listed sources, an awesome compendium of others' research and publication over many years. Amply furnished with drink recipes of the Roaring Twenties, this book does not claim encyclopedic inclusiveness, but presents its cocktails as lenses on the times. The recipes appear intact, gaining full significance from their cultural context, and the author begs indulgence if a few "favorites" have slipped past. Sources for the recipes are to be found in the volumes listed below and selected online from competing bartenders' and distillers' preferred ingredients, proportions, and preparations.

Once again, artist Julia Mills has enlivened a distinct cocktail era, this time to give the Jazz Age its unique visual "flavor" with numerous images that redouble readers' experience of print and pictures. Thank you, Ms. Mills!

Ms. Inge Klaps, a native of Belgium, has kindly typed sections of the manuscript and admits that her interest has been piqued in America's peculiar episode, Prohibition.

BIBLIOGRAPHY

Albritton, Laura, and Jerry Wilkinson. *Hidden History of the Florida Keys.*
Charleston, SC: History Press, 2018.

Allen, Everett S. *The Black Ships: Rum-Runners of Prohibition.* Boston: Little,
Brown, 1965.

Allen, Frederick Lewis. *Only Yesterday: An Informal History of the 1920s.* 1931.
Reprint: New York: HarperCollins, 1964.

Anderson, Jervis. *This Was Harlem, 1900–1950.* New York: Farrar, Straus
and Giroux, 1982.

Asbury, Herbert. *The Great Illusion: An Informal History of Prohibition.*
Garden City, NY: Doubleday, 1950.

Bair, Deirdre. *Capone: His Life, Legacy, and Legend.* New York: Anchor
Books, 2016.

Baker, James W. *Thanksgiving: The Biography of an American Institution.*
Hanover: University of New Hampshire Press, 2009.

Barbican, James [pseud.]. *The Confessions of a Rum-Runner.* 1928. Reprint.
Mystic, CT: Flat Hammock Press, 2007.

Barry, John M. *The Great Influenza: The Epic Story of the Deadliest Plague in History.* 2004. Reprint. New York: Penguin, 2005.

Barrymore, Ethel. *Memories: An Autobiography.* New York: Harper & Brothers, 1955.

Batterberry, Michael, and Ariane Batterberry. *On the Town in New York from 1776 to the Present.* New York: Charles Scribner's Sons, 1973.

Bent, Silas. *Ballyhoo: The Voice of the Press.* New York: Boni and Liveright, 1927.

Bergreen, Laurence. *Capone: The Man and the Era.* 1994. Reprint. New York: Touchstone, 1996.

Boyd, Ernest. *Portraits: Real and Imaginary.* New York: George H. Doran, 1924.

Breslin, Jimmy. *Damon Runyon: A Life.* New York: Ticknor and Fields, 1991.

Buhle, Mari Jo, Paul Buhle, and Dan Georgakas, eds. *Encyclopedia of the American Left.* 1990. Reprint. Urbana and Chicago: University of Illinois Press, 1992.

Butler, Susan. *East to the Dawn: The Life of Amelia Earhart.* 1997. Reprint. New York: Da Capo, 1999.

Carse, Robert. *Rum Row: The Liquor Fleet That Fueled the Roaring Twenties.* 1959. Reprint. Mystic, CT: Flat Hammock Press, 2007.

Chapman, Robert L. *American Slang.* New York: Harper and Row, 1987.

Chopin, Kate. *The Awakening.* 1899. Reprint. New York: Norton, 1999.

Churchwell, Sarah. *Careless People: Murder, Mayhem, and the Invention of The Great Gatsby.* New York: Penguin, 2014.

Clines, Sally. *Zelda Fitzgerald: Her Voice in Paradise.* New York: Arcade, 2002.

Craddock, Harry. *The Savoy Cocktail Book.* 1930. Reprint. Girard & Stewart, 2015.

Crockett, Albert S. *The Old Waldorf-Astoria Bar Book.* 1935. Reprint. Lightning Source UK, 2018.

Crosby, Alfred W. *America's Forgotten Pandemic: The Influenza of 1918.* 1976. Reprint. New York: Cambridge University Press, 1989.

Cross, Gary. *An All-Consuming Century: Why Commercialism Won in Modern America.* New York: Columbia University Press, 2000.

Crowninshield, Francis, ed. *Vogue's First Reader.* Garden City, NY: Halcyon House, 1944.

Dos Passos, John. *The Big Money.* 1933. Reprint. New York: Houghton Mifflin, 1974.

———. *Manhattan Transfer.* 1925. Reprint. New York: Penguin, 1986.

———. *1919.* 1932. Reprint. New York: Houghton Mifflin, 2000.

Duncan, Isadora. *My Life.* New York: Liveright, 1927.

Erenberg, Lewis A. *Steppin' Out: New York Nightlife and the Transformation of American Culture, 1890–1930.* 1981. Reprint. Chicago: University of Chicago Press: 1984.

Fitzgerald, F. Scott. *The Beautiful and Damned.* 1922. Reprint. New York: Barnes & Noble, 2005.

———. *The Great Gatsby.* 1925. Reprint. New York: Collier, 1992.

———. *The Letters of F. Scott Fitzgerald.* New York: Charles Scribner's Sons, 1963.

———. *Six Tales of the Jazz Age and Other Stories.* New York: Charles Scribner's Sons, 1950.

———. *The Short Stories of F. Scott Fitzgerald.* New York: Scribner's, 1989.

———. *This Side of Paradise.* 1920. Reprint. New York: Charles Scribner's Sons, 1954.

Fitzgerald, Zelda. *The Collected Writings of Zelda Fitzgerald.* Tuscaloosa: University of Alabama Press, 1991.

———. *Save Me the Waltz.* 1932. Reprint. London: Vintage, 2001.

Foy, Jessica H., and Thomas J. Schlereth, eds. *American Home Life, 1880–1930*. 1992. Reprint. Knoxville: University of Tennessee Press, 1994.

Geisst, Charles R. *Wall Street: A History from Its Beginnings to the Fall of Enron*. New York: Oxford University Press, 1997.

Gilman, Charlotte Perkins. *Herland*. 1909–16. Reprint. New York: Pantheon, 1979.

Grandi, Piero. *Cocktails*. Rome, Italy, 1927.

Greene, Philip. *To Have and Have Another: A Hemingway Cocktail Companion*. New York: Perigree, 2015.

Hampton, Dan. *The Flight: Charles Linbergh's Daring and Immortal 1927 Transatlantic Crossing*. New York: HarperCollins, 2017.

Haskell, Arlo. *The Jews of Key West: Smugglers, Cigar Makers, and Revolutionaries (1823–1969)*. Key West, FL: Sandpaper Press, 2017.

Hays, Arthur Garfield. *Let Freedom Ring*. New York: Liveright, 1937.

Hemingway, Ernest. *A Farewell to Arms*. 1929. Reprint. New York: Charles Scribner's Sons, 1957.

———. *In Our Time*. 1925. Reprint. New York: Charles Scribner's Sons, 1953.

———. *A Moveable Feast*. 1964. Reprint. New York: Scribner, 2010.

———. *The Sun Also Rises*. 1926. Reprint. New York: Charles Scribner's Sons, 1954.

Herald, Jacqueline. *Fashions of a Decade: The 1920s*. New York: Chelsea House, 2007.

Kellner, Bruce, ed. *The Harlem Renaissance: A Historical Dictionary for the Era*. New York: Methuen, 1987.

Lender, Mark Edward, and James Kirby Martin. *Drinking in America: A History*. New York: Free Press, 1987.

Lewis, David Levering. *When Harlem Was in Vogue*. New York: Vintage, 1982.

Lewis, Sinclair. *Babbitt*. 1922. Reprint. New York: Penguin, 1996.

———. *Dodsworth.* 1929. Reprint. New York: New American Library, 1972.

Lindbergh, Anne Morrow. *North to the Orient.* New York: Harcourt, Brace, & Co., 1935.

Ling, Sally J. *Run the Rum In: South Florida during Prohibition.* Charleston, SC: History Press, 2007.

MacElhone, Harry. *ABC of Mixing Cocktails.* 1930. Reprint. Eastford, CT: Martino Fine Books, 2017.

Mackrell, Judith. *Flappers: Six Women of a Dangerous Generation.* New York: Farrar, Straus and Giroux, 2013.

Marling, Karal Ann. *Merry Christmas!: Celebrating America's Greatest Holiday.* Cambridge, MA: Harvard University Press, 2000.

Marquis, Don. *The Old Soak and Hail and Farewell.* Garden City, NY: Doubleday, Page & Company, 1921.

May, Lary. *Screening Out the Past: The Birth of Mass Culture and the Motion Picture Industry.* New York: Oxford University Press, 1980.

Meier, Frank. *The Artistry of Mixing Drinks.* 1936. Reprint. New York: Mud Puddle Books, 2009.

Menand, Louis. "When Ballplayers First Became Stars." *New Yorker,* June 1, 2020: 54–59.

Mencken, H. L. *Prejudices: A Selection.* New York: Vintage, 1958.

———. *The Vintage Mencken.* New York: Vintage, 1955.

Merz, Charles. *The Dry Decade.* 1930. Reprint. Seattle: University of Washington Press, 1969.

Meyers, Jeffrey. *Hemingway: A Biography.* New York: Routledge, 1985.

Milford, Nancy. *Zelda: A Biography.* New York: Harper & Row, 1970.

Mott, Frank Luther. *A History of American Magazines, vol. V: 1905–1930.* Cambridge, MA: Harvard University Press, 1968.

Mowry, George E., Editor. *The Twenties: Fords, Flappers & Fanatics.* Englewood Cliffs, NJ: Prentice Hall, 1963.

Murdock, Catherine Gilbert. *Domesticating Drink: Women, Men, and Alcohol in America, 1870–1940.* Baltimore: Johns Hopkins University Press, 1998.

Parker, Dorothy. *The Portable Dorothy Parker*. New York: Penguin, 1976.

Reynolds, Michael. *Hemingway: The Paris Years*. 1989. Reprint. New York: Norton, 1999.

Rich, Doris L. *Amelia Earhart: A Biography*. New York: Dell, 1989.

The Roaring '20s: Flappers, Bootleggers, Gangsters, Suffragists. New York: New York Times, 2019.

Roff, Benny. *Speakeasy: 200 Underground Cocktails*. London: Hardie Grant Books, 2015.

Runyon, Damon. *A Treasury of Damon Runyon*. New York: Modern Library, 1958.

Schoenberg, Robert J. *Mr. Capone: The Real—and Complete—Story of Al Capone*. New York: HarperCollins, 1992.

Seldes, Gilbert. *The Future of Drinking*. Boston: Little, Brown, 1930.

———. *The Seven Lively Arts*. New York: Harper & Brothers, 1924.

Shearer, Victoria. *It Happened in the Florida Keys*. Guilford, CT: TwoDot, 2007.

Sinclair, Upton. *Oil!* New York: Grosset & Dunlap, 1927.

Sklar, Robert. *Movie-Made America: A Cultural History of American Movies*. 1975. Reprint. New York: Vintage, 1994.

Sullivan, Edward D. *Rattling the Cup on Chicago Crime*. New York: Vanguard Press, 1929.

Sullivan, Mark. *Our Times: The Twenties*. 1935. Reprint. New York: Charles Scribner's Sons, 1972.

Tindall, George Brown, and David Shi. *America: A Narrative History*. New York: W.W. Norton, 1984.

Vreeland, Diana. *D.V.* 1984. Reprint. New York: Ecco, 2011.

Whitman, Walt. *November Boughs*. 1888. Reprint. Mineola, NY: Dover, 2014.

Willard, Frances. *Occupations for Women*. New York: Success Company, 1897.

Wilson, Edmund. *The American Earthquake: A Chronicle of the Roaring Twenties, the Great Depression, and the Dawn of the New Deal.* 1958. Reprint. New York: De Capo, 1996.

Winters, Kathleen C. *Anne Morrow Lindbergh: First Lady of the Air.* New York: Palgrave Macmillan, 2006.

Zeitz, Joshua. *Flapped: A Madcap Story of Sex, Style, Celebrity, and the Women Who Made America Modern.* New York: Alfred A. Knopf, 1971.

INDEX OF COCKTAIL RECIPES

Alexander Cocktail, 17
Arnold Rothstein Cocktail, 64
The Asbach Cocktail, 112
The Automobile Cocktail, 82
The Aviation Cocktail, 114

Bacardi Cocktail, 91
Bee's Knees, 69
Bela Lugosi Cocktail, 129
Bloody Mary (à la Ernest
    Hemingway), 78
Boulevardiere Cocktail, 116-117
Brandy and Soda, 79
The Bronx, 15
Buried in Clover, 140

Cameron's Kick Cocktail, 98
Capone Cocktail, 34-35

The Cat's Pajamas, 68
Champagne Cocktail, 77
Champagne Julep, 97
Charlie Chaplin Cocktail, 127
Chocolate Cocktail, 16
Christmas Punch Hot, 135
Clover Club Cocktail, 64
Colonial Cocktail, 17

Dance the Charleston Cocktail, 56
Detroit River Crossing, 35
Dorothy Gish Cocktail, 127

Everything's "Jake," 91

Fairbanks Cocktail, 126
Fishing Trip, 90-91
The Flapper Cocktail, 55

Foreign Correspondent Cocktail, 118

Four Flusher, 67

Gin Rickey, 77

Glühwein, 78

Goldfish Cocktail, 43

Harry MacElhone's 1920s Paris Recipe, 118

Havana Smile, 98

High Hat, 140

Horsefeathers, 69

Hot Rum Punch, 78-79

It Cocktail, 45

Journalist Cocktail, 117

Kingston Cooler, 92

Lindbergh Crossing, 113

Lipstick Cocktail, 63

Live Wire Cocktail, 56

Making Whoopee, 46

Manhattan, 16

Mary Pickford Cocktail, 126-127

Martini, 16

Millionaire Cocktail, 139

Nineteen-Twenty Cocktail, 18

Old Fashion(ed), 112

On All Sixes, 70

On a Toot, 68

Orange Blossom, 77

Orange Satchmo, 63

Original Gangster, 35

"Pappy" Chalk, 113

Petting Pantry, 44-45

Rich Daddy, 140

St. Valentine's Day Massacre, 37

Says You!, 68

Scofflaw Cocktail, 117

Scotch and Soda, 112

Sheik Highball, 44

Sidecar Cocktail, 62-63

Snorky's Kiss, 37

Soul Kiss, 45

Take the Nickel, 36

Tax Evasion, 38

Theda Bara Cocktail, 129

Tommy Gun, 36-37

To the Lost, 79

TNT, 36

Twelve Miles Out, 90

Valentino, 44

Volstead Cocktail, 17